Beyond the Twelve Steps

Other Books by Lynn Grabhorn

Excuse Me, Your Life *Is Waiting*

The Excuse Me, Your Life Is Waiting *Playbook*

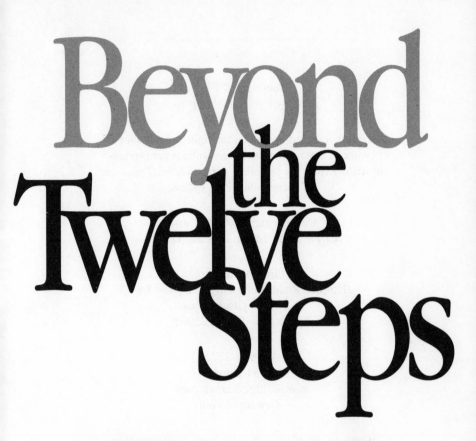

Beyond the Twelve Steps

roadmap to a new life

lynn grabhorn

HAMPTON ROADS
PUBLISHING COMPANY, INC.

Cover design by Garn Turner
Cover art by Turner Type and Design

For information write:
Hampton Roads Publishing Company, Inc.
1125 Stoney Ridge Road
Charlottesville, VA 22902

434-296-2772
fax: 434-296-5096
e-mail: hrpc@hrpub.com
www.hrpub.com

If you are unable to order this book from your local
bookseller, you may order directly from the publisher.
Call 1-800-766-8009, toll-free.

Library of Congress Catalog Card Number: 00-111727

ISBN 1-57174-267-0

10 9 8 7 6 5 4 3

Printed on acid-free paper in Canada

DEDICATION

Many magnificent beings have provided the inspiration for these pages, and I can't begin to adequately express my gratitude. Yet there is one who took me by the nape of my frozen image and force-fed me straight into that fervent, unswerving desire to go beyond. He's a crafty old goat who has stopped at nothing to teach me love of Self. He has pushed, prodded, manipulated, scolded, infuriated, and loved me beyond possible measure. To him, my first teacher whom I love as Life itself, I appreciatively and reverently dedicate this book.

CONTENTS

ACKNOWLEDGMENTS

Without sobriety, not only would this new journey be impossible, but I rather doubt I'd be here to take it. So my first and deepest thanks goes to Alcoholics Anonymous and those grand, hard-nosed old-timers of my early sobriety in Hollywood. Of course, anyone with a few days on the Program was an old-timer to me then, like Eddie, who I didn't know from Adam and had about two months at the time. Every night, for the first thirty days of my sobriety, he'd appear at my door to take me to a meeting. And I'd go. How often I've wondered if I would have made it had it not been for Eddie. And Mary Pat, my sponsor, who listened for hours on end to my ramblings, offering just the right words to get me out of my own stumbling way. Chuck C., Clancy, Alabam, Polly Hall, just old-time names to most, but names that meant life to me.

In more recent times, I want to deeply acknowledge Jale Greenlief for her inspiring contribution to the foundations of Adult Children of Alcoholics. Her intense eight-week workshop, in my twenty-third year on A.A., was the turning point which freed me to follow this new path.

And I want to extend a very special thanks to a unique group of men and women who have made so many of these grand teachings available to tens of thousands around the world. While this is only a small portion of the list, among those whom I particularly want to thank are Jane Roberts, who channeled all of the Seth books; J. Z. Knight, who channels Ramtha; Jackie Snyder, who channels Zarathustra; Penny Torres, who channels Mafu; Ken Carey, who channels all manner of cosmic beings; and most of all, Didi Carstens, who channels, among others, Rajni.

Many patient souls extended a hand in editing this book. My friend Joan Babcock from Wisconsin came to Washington for six weeks to work on editing. Didi Carstens gave me a major hand in rewriting a couple of difficult chapters. My sister, Mary Yoder, offered suggestions from the very first draft, while both Kathy Hawn and Julie Shorten helped me to see some different perspectives. In fact, to all who have so lovingly assisted in this project go my deepest thanks and appreciation, beginning first and foremost with Bill W. and Doctor Bob!

CHAPTER 1
THAT PRECIOUS REUNION

You have some "time" on the Program. Or, as one might say in more casual circles, you've "been around" a while. You're at that stage where on one hand newcomers look up to you as someone who's "been there," and on the other, you feel you can finally hold your own in a conversation with those blasted, beloved "old timers."

And what's the Program? Well, it could be any one of the dozens of Twelve-Step Programs to which millions of us now attribute a better life, or even being alive. Or both. Alcoholics Anonymous, Cocaine Anonymous, Al-Anon, Narcotics Anonymous, Adult Children of Alcoholics, Alateen, Nicotine Anonymous, Debtors Anonymous, or You-Name-It-Anonymous; if you've ever sat through a bunch of meetings in some grungy church basement and heard, "Rarely have we seen a person fail who has thoroughly followed these steps . . . ," you're a Twelve-Stepper.

You feel fairly comfortable on the Program most of the time. Not great, really, but OK, except for that relentless gnawing. No matter; you have a moderately good relationship with your Higher

Power, you speak at meetings off and on, and you probably still have one or two "babies" or "pigeons," those newcomers who incessantly bug you on the other end of a phone.

Basically, you've got it together. You're sober, or clean, or in a process of releasing, slimming, whatever. You feel pretty good about your Program on the whole. You go to an acceptable number of meetings, take a good Tenth Step now and then, and may even opt for some occasional Twelfth-Step work when pressed. A model member. But this feeling that there's something more just won't leave you alone. Ninety percent of the time you're not even aware of it, but that other ten percent, what *is* it?

You go about your life pretty much by rote. You wake up in the morning not flying, but OK, and hit work with the same "hi" to the same boss every day. You dutifully reach for that scrungy coffee cup with your name on it and begin your workday after the usual complaints about the coffee's quality. You listen to the same, unfunny jokes from the bunch, laugh at the appropriate spots (God forbid you shouldn't be one of the troops!), and make the obligatory comments about Susie's new dress and how low it's cut.

Nothing changes, particularly you. There's no excitement, no newness. Maybe you should get more involved with the Program again, maybe get more newcomers to work with, or put in some hours down at Central Office. Maybe it's time for another inventory. Damn! What *is* it?

Then come the long walks. Are you really looking for something, or is it just spring fever in January? A new church, or dance group, or study group, anything new to fill that void.

Perhaps you should share the feeling at a meeting? No, you guess not. How can you talk about a feeling when you don't even know what the feeling is you're feeling?

So what is it? If you really tried, could you put your finger on it? Empty? Lonely? Or just basically unjazzed? Of course, you don't want to look at it too closely because it might be nothing more than midlife crisis or college doldrums.

Then again, maybe your situation isn't so subtle. Maybe you're one of the "Dear-God-how-did-I-ever-get-myself-into-this-mess-and-if-it-doesn't-change-soon-I'm-going-to-kill-myself" group. And you go to meetings, smiling your usual answer to the usual greetings, "Oh, fine, thanks. I'm just fine."

You keep stuffing the feelings as unrecognizable. After all, you're sober, or clean, or releasing, or off cigarettes and card tables, aren't you? What else is important? Finally, in shoulder-shrugging resignation, you conclude it's probably nothing. After all, your life is a damn sight better than it was before the Program, and isn't that what it's all about?

No! That kind of thinking won't work any longer. Everything is not fine, not by a long shot. By capping your feelings, denying what the magnificent inner voice within you is trying to scream into your sleeping consciousness, you're simply stuffing them farther down to fester yet another day. No, this is definitely not what life is all about.

THE FEELING OF ALONENESS

Most of us go through life not knowing what we want but being pretty darn sure this isn't it. So we walk around with that gnawing feeling of aloneness. Oh sure, we believe in a Higher Power—out *there*. We know it's always there, ready to interact with us the moment we call to it. But the problem is we're forever removing ourselves from that *conscious contact* and reverting right back to where we were—empty, separate.

Since we're certain it would be impossible to stay "plugged in" every second of every day, the Higher Power gets put on the back burner, ready for duty when called upon. We go on picking up scraps of joy here and there in those rare and wonderful moments of carefree living, those moments of what? Ahh, those moments of not feeling *alone*!

That Magnificent Longing

How much of a surprise would it be to learn that the purpose of life was to live, to be *really alive*, to be filled with the adventure of all life, to be in absolute control of your own destiny, to be a joyous learner from life, loving every moment of the ride? Life was designed to be a platform for us to live our creativity, to live and express our individuality in colorful and challenging ways simply because those things bring us joy.

For most of us, however, the purpose of life has been earning the dollar, finding the "right" relationship, getting the house, making it work. Little have we known that all those things we've been working at, and going through, are nothing more than roadmaps from the soul. What do you think that longing is that's been pounding inside of you? It's the soul of your Being pleading with you to opt for something more vast, pleading with you to end this experiment in frozen living. "Wake up," it's saying. "You don't know who you are! Wake up and find out! I won't let up until you do! Wake up, damn it, *wake up*!"

A light goes on. Something in you knows what to do, where to look. You find new books like this one, new people, new groups. You feel as if a door has opened and fresh breezes are blowing through. You're beginning to feed that magnificent longing. New life is stirring in you, and your journey to a place inside we'll call "Home" has just begun.

You've been homesick for that Home, though you can't remember it. You can't remember because it's too vast to fit into your present structure of thought. You've been wanting something, but you haven't known what. And if you're at all like me, there's been an increasing urgency attached to that desire. And so here you are, about to begin this most incredible of all journeys.

Take care. If you don't want your world rocked, your security shaken, or your tidy little sandbox disturbed, you may not want to spend time in these pages. Some of the concepts may startle you, or even frighten you. But stay with it and give that longing a chance. Let yourself drink in answers to questions as old as time itself: who you are, what you are, why you are. This is not power of positive thinking, although that's involved. Nor is it cosmic razzle-dazzle. What's in this book is truth as I have learned it, truth that has totally changed my life and the lives of thousands.

So let your journey begin! It's the reawakening of what you've always known but long forgotten. You pack your Twelve Steps and take them with you. You are on your road Home, that warm place of remembrance that's been calling to you for so long, that place inside holding total knowledge of who and what you are. It's your God within standing up, shaking itself off, and beginning to smile.

FREEDOM: THE INSIDE JOB

Imagine what it would be like to have no cares, no worries, no anxieties, but to just *be* in the face of whatever's going on, to welcome the experience of pain, to acknowledge fear, and do all this within a world of ease and serenity, instead of raving panic.

Tough to imagine, isn't it? Right now you're probably quite right in thinking such a utopia couldn't possibly exist. Yet once you come to accept one simple principle in your life, you'll see how possible it is. That principle is simply to know, *to know*, you have choices. And not only do you have choices, but you have within you an energy center more powerful than ten thousand suns to make those choices happen.

There are two essential points to absorb before you can move on. If you feel resistance to them, simply acknowledge that resistance and keep going, for these points set the stage for an easier opening of the doors within which have been locked for so long. These two points are:

> *1) You will never know the elixir of the freedom of life that is your birthright as long as you are addicted to the idea that manipulating your universe from the outside will make you happy.*

> *2) Nothing, nothing, will change in your life until you absolutely know that you are worth more than you are now getting.*

Two toughies, no question about it. The first, because we've been taught to believe in outside circumstances since babyhood; the second, because beliefs about our worth (or lack of it) are buried so deeply we have no idea they even exist.

SHINY NEW TOOLS

How often have you had a flash that this thing you see as you is a whole lot bigger than one could perceive? We've all had those feelings but usually stuffed them, lest such outrageous thinking rock our already shaky boat.

The fact is, we are far more than we think we are, vaster, more magnificent, and more powerful than the tiny, minute knowledge of ourselves can presently imagine. If you let it, that vastness will be your inner teacher, reaching out to you with golden keys of freedom. The secret in letting it happen lies in understanding the physics behind this vastness. That's right, physics! Energy! Force! Power!

You don't have to keep repeating the same, negative experiences over and over and wonder why. You don't have to repeat the same problems with lifemates, and jobs, and money, and wonder why. You don't have to, unless you want to. You have choices, wonderful, amazing choices.

Be open to the reality that you are not a mere, limited being of flesh and blood but rather a center of energy filled with life and power, a vortex of such immense force that, once harnessed, you are able to change your life in whatever manner you desire, whenever you desire to do so.

FROM CHAPTER ONE TO CHAPTER TWO

Sometimes we take our Twelve Steps for granted; other times we're overwhelmed with gratitude for their simple power. Sometimes we work them; other times we ignore them. But at no time have we ever left them, no matter how often we may have slipped or stumbled. They are part of us forever, for nothing, but nothing, could ever replace those magnificent Twelve Steps.

The principles within these pages are not intended to replace anything. They are new. They go beyond. From Chapter One, now comes Chapter Two, so to speak. In Chapter One, our Program, we established ourselves as functional members of society, no longer chained to the addictions of our existence. The more we got into the Twelve Steps and "practiced them in all our affairs," the more serenity inched into our lives, giving us the freedom to reach for more. And now, we're ready for chapter Two.

FOLLOW THE CALL

Home is that place inside where God is, that place inside we've longed for, but forgotten. Until we're at least open to believing this self we inhabit is only a fraction of what we really are, until we realize the sun and the ocean are as nothing beside us, and until we can give up the idea that God is something separate from us, that longing inside will never leave, and we'll be going around in the same unfulfilled circles for the rest of our lives.

What we're going for here is simply a process of waking up. There are no rules, and there is no rush. Everyone gets it when they get it. So, as you go through the coming pages, do so with a sense of allowing, without judgment. Be willing to entertain new beliefs, new insights, new ways of thinking. The more open you are to these truths, the more rapidly your life will change, for the more rapidly *you* will change.

You'll be embarking on a journey as ancient and as natural as life itself, and one hundred percent guaranteed. Whether you dive in with an insatiable hunger and go at breakneck speed or lightly sample bits and pieces of the smorgasbord as it passes before you, you'll never again be able to return to what you are now, nor will you want to.

With just a little willingness, you can leave your old ways, hurts, and struggles behind and opt for the life, love, and wisdom your soul so desperately yearns to experience. That's the longing you feel, the yearning, the call for you to remember all of what you really are. Let it be. Follow your yearning. All those defenses you've so carefully built are beginning to weaken, and the floodgates are pushing open with the strength of your desire to know. Coming forth is what you've been looking for all your life.

ROADMAP TO WHERE? JOURNEY TO WHAT?

Alcoholic that I am, punch lines are dear to me. With the thought that you, too, may have this same trait, I felt an overview of where this road is leading might be helpful.

While you'll find within these pages an easy-to-follow roadmap, you'll also run across some subjects which are basically unprovable. For instance, no one to my knowledge has yet been able to prove God. Nor has anyone been able to prove what's contained in the subconscious, or that prayer is heard, or that every human being owns powers beyond imagination. That a great deal of evidential data exists on the qualities of thought and its electromagnetic properties is about as close as I can come to offering any kind of proof that some of the things we're going to be talking about are verifiable. For the most part, they're not.

However, most of us who are now thrilling to this new way of life don't even think about proof. The knowledge we're accumulating is resonating so deeply in our Beings, and causing such dramatic changes in our lives, we just live it and want more!

What's written here is what I've learned, felt, experienced, witnessed, believed, and become since beginning this "wake-up" process. If it rings bells within you, you'll know it, for your whole

Being will shout with joy to the heavens. If not, so be it. And if, down the road, you're still wondering if there isn't something more, just come on back. It will never be too late to begin this journey to a new life.

DISCOVERING THE SOMETHING MORE

The trip starts for most of us with the same reasons you picked up this book . . . wanting something more than just surviving. We gradually move into a new concept of ourselves as spiritual beings and begin to get the first real inklings that the only force creating our reality is us. That's shocking, maybe even frightening at first, but eventually we get used to the idea.

Finally it sinks in; *we can't separate ourselves from what we already are!* We realize we're just as much a piece of God as a leaf is of its tree. Separation from our Source, the "God-there-Me-here" syndrome, is just not something we can live with any longer.

Before long, we come to see that the something more we seek is ourSelves (the capitol *S* keynotes our divinity), Selves that are more than anything we could possibly imagine, or have ever known. Bit by bit, we walk into a new and immensely loving relationship with the Source of our Being, God, All That Is, our Higher Power within and without.

You actually feel this union. Then it dawns on you; you're not taking this journey alone and never have. The God of your being has walked with you, guided you, and loved you beyond measure since time began and before.

We're learning that love is not something you do, but something you are, that it is our very essence, our core. A major part of our journey is learning how to reach in, touch, and ignite that precious inner core.

This journey beyond the Twelve Steps is bringing our union with God into fruition.

JUST CHOP WOOD

There's an old Eastern parable that tells of the fellow, a woodcutter by trade, who became enlightened after studying for years with masters of high spiritual learning. His friends, quite confounded by the devotion he displayed to his studies, asked of him what he intended to do after he became enlightened. With sensible logic he replied, "Chop wood; what else?"

The purpose of opening to this new life is not to build a holy temple in which to sit and contemplate our navels forevermore but to live as we have never lived before. We find that life is the grandest gift there is. Instead of trudging its road of happy destiny, we take on life as the greatest lover we have ever had.

We're in partnership, in cocreation, with our Source, the All That Is, our Higher Power, God. It's an absolute, glorious partnership in which we learn to give up the priority of being unhappy.

No longer beholden to our past, or to an uncertain future, we learn to get into the *moment of now* and stay there. A dearly loved member of my home group used to say, "If you keep one eye on yesterday, and one eye on tomorrow, you'll be cockeyed today." Great expression and I loved it, but actually living it was quite another matter until beginning this new way of life. Learning to live in the now, we find the exquisite joy of simply chopping wood, no matter how tough the knots.

TAKING BACK OUR POWER

That we were powerless over our addiction is hardly a topic for argument, for our ego-selves gave the addiction that power. But this has never meant we were powerless, period, not by a long shot.

We come to see that almost every day of our lives we've given our power away to someone, or something, to govern us. And what did we lose in those transactions? Love of ourselves, therefore, love of God. Every time we gave our power away, we fanned the illusion of separation from our reality. The aloneness, the longing, just went on and on.

Then comes the dawn. If we're no longer giving all of our power away, we must still have it within us. Gradually, a day at a time, we begin to use the power we had so unknowingly given to everyone and everything but ourselves. Miracles begin to happen; our lives begin to change. It's a wild, free, indescribable feeling of joy, humility, power, and oneness.

AND THINGS LIKE . . .

Living this way of life is truly getting rid of pain, not to mention struggle. It doesn't mean we won't have lessons, or what I call "fires," to go through. We will, and do. But can you imagine going through a mess with ease? Can you imagine being laid off and being honestly grateful for the lesson?

We learn how to stop clinging to things and people. Then the courage to allow happiness comes, because we learn how to ask for it, demand it, and create it.

And what's happiness? To me, now, it's having all of my needs met. As to joy, well, that's creating my wants, and having them met! You learn what it means to live in joy, how to please your own heart and soul, how to be yourself, totally. And it all really happens, bringing incredible, indescribable happiness.

Remember, these are the *results* of embarking on this journey, not the "how to's." And if all of this sounds impossible, I understand. And yet it's not impossible. These same results have happened to me and thousands like me, ordinary, devoted Program people who couldn't understand why life kept batting them over the head with the same old hammer time after time.

We found there *is* more to this life. Things like no longer needing to look outside ourselves for our happiness (and no longer kidding ourselves we don't really do this). Things like enjoying, I mean really enjoying, being by ourselves now and then, or permanently. Enjoying sitting and just being, without having to fill a screaming void with the stereo, or TV, or telephone, or even a book.

Things such as beginning to trust, developing a calm awareness that life's under control, no matter what's flying around. You're in the flow, allowing life's lessons to happen, allowing life to live you.

OWNING IT ALL

To learn that everything we've ever done, we've done because we wanted to, and that whatever we are, we created by ourselves, is not always easy to swallow. We learn to accept how we've created our life, and how to change it. In part, that means giving up blame of any sort. It means owning that we've designed how we live.

If we're walking through life filled with unhappiness, worry, self-pity, misery, loneliness, self-denial, we come to see how we bring these things about and own that realization, removing blame totally from any other person, place, or thing, past or present. It's realizing we've created our life by how we think!

When we finally acknowledge, deep within, that we have indeed created our own reality, our past no longer owns us; rather, it becomes part of our wisdom. Our hates, resentments, and fears no longer push our buttons, and, best of all, no longer control our future.

As so we take back our power; our lives begin to change. The new bounce to our step is seen by all, especially by us.

ALLOWING THE HAPPINESS

With the understanding of how we have given away our power and allowed our lives to be created and ruled by our own uncontrolled thinking, we search for the next obvious step: turning our thoughts around.

When we came to our Twelve-Step Program, it didn't take long for us to find out that until we took our all-important First Step, we weren't going to get very far. For some, the First Step was a relief. For others, it was agony. Either way, once that was under our belts, the door opened to a new world.

So it is with the steps to awakening that sleeping giant within us. "First things first" means accepting we do indeed create our own reality and how that happens. Gradually, almost magically, we begin to manifest the outrageous realities we've always wanted in our lives as we learn to work with the universal energies, within and without, as one.

HOME TO UNLIMITED

There are streams of moments on this journey that are so sweet, so empowering, so awe-inspiring, that when things go awry, as they often do, you will have stored an enormous reserve of awareness and love from which to draw. Thus the impact of the fires, or problems, is greatly cushioned, and solutions come quickly. Of course, just as on the Program, the faster we grow in the skills of mastery, the less the impact of each succeeding fire.

Then, as the flames of self-love expand, there comes an insatiable hunger for more. And why not? When was the last time you felt warmed, loved, held, caressed, rocked, soothed, understood, accepted, approved of, enjoyed, cared for, cherished, valued, appreciated, treasured, and adored, all at the same time, by or from your own Self?

We come to allow that delicious love from our Inner Being, the energy of the universe which courses through every atom of our cells. We learn to tap into that power and merge with it, for it is our very essence! With the tapping-in comes a feeling of alignment, of being-in-touch-with. It may last for only a few seconds, maybe longer, but you never forget it.

And then you grow into a new kind of oneness with life where you experience love without personality, where you acquire a wisdom without superiority, and where you experience power without arrogance. And you're alive. Oh God, you're so alive!

So, does this mean you're going to put a halo around your head and walk off into Never-Never Land without ever again having to trip over another difficulty? Hardly! What it does mean is that you can learn how to give no power to problems and move directly to another level of where solutions can be quickly manifested. Before long, problems actually become exciting and welcome challenges from which to learn.

Defenses drop. Tensions fall away. Frustrations take a back seat. Hopelessness vanishes. You discover there's a purpose to your life and how to fulfill that purpose. I think the proper words are "finding yourself," and oh, how sweet it is!

It's happening all around the globe today, people waking up to know who, what, and why they really are; people seeing themselves as unlimited centers of God-energy, rather than vulnerable human beings; people learning the challenging but beautiful process of allowing, rather than judging; people removing all fear and unfolding from limitation into unlimitedness, a day at a time.

Above all, this is a journey of stretching our minds, bending our consciousness, pushing our thoughts so high and so hard our brains hurt—literally—then stretching farther still to open our minds to even greater understandings, and learning how to live those understandings a day at a time.

Of course, to become the unlimited beings we were designed to be means change. For most of us, that is definitely not a process we look upon with relish. The old is being pulled away to make room for the new, another level, another attitude, another perception, and it's not always sunshine and roses.

We ask for help from the power within and without, and change happens. It happens with a new strength, gentleness, and love that's blossoming within us, even in the midst of our fears.

One of the biggest fears we confront is loss of our past (our identity) and of the emotions which those memories bring. And perhaps the greatest freedom we confront is the loss of our guilt in doing what bring us joy, *and then doing it!*

As our courage grows, we begin to manifest new events, people, and circumstances in our lives. It feels as if new energy is dancing in our circuitry, because we're in a different space, a different level of consciousness, operating at a different frequency.

Life becomes filled with expectations because we know how to call those expectations forth, knowing darn good and well there's nothing wrong with doing it. We claim our right to be happy and create that happiness. As one of my favorite teachers says, "If it's not fun, it's not worth your Godhood!"

TOOLS FOR THE JOURNEY

We came into this life loaded with every kind of tool imaginable to help our wake-up process begin. But somehow we forgot; we forgot the powers we were given. We forgot at the deepest level and have been on a lifelong search for we knew not what.

Within these pages are the keys to awaken yourself to the powerful tools within you, as well as basic directions on how to use them. Some of the tools are unlocked by taking actual steps, others through golden understandings. They go together, steps and understandings. Some have to do with the nature of thought, others with learning how to take back the magnificent power we've so thoughtlessly given away.

These steps are nothing more than helping hands in the journey back to God. Your path will be as natural for you as mine has been for me. Wherever you are this moment, you have only to ask that the wisdom come to you, and signposts will begin to appear that say, "This way. Here's your roadmap. It's been a long journey. Come on. Come *Home*."

Not a thing along the way can hurt you. The God of your Being along with all the forces of the universe dearly want you to remember and will go to unimaginable lengths to give you safe, loving assistance.

No, we are not alone on this journey, nor have we ever been! Let yourself get into the flow, into the exquisite process of realizing what you already are. Make up your mind there is nothing to keep you from delicious happiness and joy, or from just old-fashioned peace and contentment, or from finding out how deserving you are to have it all!

And then the day comes when you find yourself sitting somewhere in your own special place. The wind is at your back, and the breezes are blowing through your hair in gentle abandon. All is at peace within you. And the tears come. You don't really understand the tears, but you allow them. It's as if you've just come back to you after a long, long absence, and the reunion is precious beyond words. And so you weep. You weep the kind of tears you have longed to weep for as long as you can remember. This is a moment you will never forget. You know you are on your road Home to the *real* you, and to a life more wondrous than you can imagine.

CHAPTER 2

THE BRIDGE TO MASTERY

"If only I had been . . . ."
"Why wasn't I ever . . . ."
"If it hadn't been for . . . ."
"I didn't have any choice over . . . ."
"If they (he/she) hadn't . . . ."
Sound familiar?

Not long after coming to the Program, we discover our addiction hasn't been our problem. We've been our own problem all along, so, with our addiction under control a day at a time, we roll up our sleeves, dig into the steps, talk hours on end with our sponsors, and start in whole hog to go to work on us.

It's a good feeling, scary at times and painful, but exciting. We know we've got hold of something as that unfamiliar feeling called hope starts slowly but surely to replace the familiar, old feelings of helplessness.

Then we notice something odd happening. As the most obvious problems caused from our addiction begin to dissolve in the face of growth, the apparently new problems springing up now seem to cling to us like mussels on shoreline rocks. Resolutely, almost defiantly, we forge ahead, waiting for time, or a change of circumstances, or even our Higher Power to bring answers. When answers don't come, or our life doesn't take on the direction we had hoped it would, more times than not we search *out there* for the reasons, hoping that our Higher Power, or a change in *them* or *that*, will create the solutions we want. And if we can't find the reasons out there, we may just throw in the towel and look *back then* for the string of causes of what's going on with us today.

This way of thinking is called, quite simply, blame. It's also called victimhood, operating from the altogether common arena known as victim mentality. Most of us have lived that way to one degree or another all our lives, usually without the foggiest idea of how consistently we blame people, places, or things for where we are in life at this moment. Rarely do we realize it's this kind of thinking which keeps us stuck in the very problems we're trying to overcome.

There's a bridge to be crossed between where we are now and where we want to go into this new expansion of self, a bridge most of us never knew existed. It's called the Bridge to Mastery. By making the conscious decision to cross it, we walk out of the world of victimhood in which we've allowed everyone else from past or present to have control over us, consciously or otherwise, and start taking control of our destiny as the divine Masters we are.

Pie in the sky? Not at all. Being an unconscious blamer has been a way of life for most of us. "If only, if only, if only." We do it without thinking. But once we cross that bridge, we leave behind the comfortable victim role where we've taken little or no responsibility for our fate. Suddenly, and often to our surprise, life starts to go the way we, and we alone, design it. We're living our God, being our own Master. And while

THE BRIDGE TO MASTERY

all it takes is a change of focus, that change is the key to finding our Godhood. It's called, simply enough, "from out there, to in here."

WHO'S RESPONSIBLE?

Here are a few basic questions you might want to answer to help set the stage for understanding the process and power of thought. Take a moment with these questions to see how often you place your focus outside yourself, how often you inadvertently think others to be the cause of your reactions, emotions, or circumstances.

There's no right or wrong to your answers. We've all lived this way to some degree before starting our wake-up process, placing responsibility for our lives in the hands of others. This is the start of understanding how we've created our world through misfocused thought, how we've fooled ourselves into thinking our choices in life were limited due to circumstances beyond our control.

You may want to take more time at a later date to do a thorough, written inventory with these questions, going into much more valuable detail and insight.

> *1) What's the primary feeling you've had over the last two or three weeks? Have you felt anxious, hurt, angry, happy? And who or what would you say is most responsible for that feeling?*
>
> *2) What are some of your main "if only's"? You know, "if only I had a better education, I could . . . ," or, "if only my parents hadn't been that way, I could . . . ," Better job, more money, different life partner, etc.,*

*etc. And again, who would you say is primarily
responsible for the perceived lacks?*

*3) When was your last "low" day, and who or what
was the reason?*

*4) What roles or images do you see yourself in today?
In a bad relationship, in a good job, too skinny,
short of money, etc.? And who is primarily
responsible?*

We all have answers to at least one or more of these questions,
for at one time or another we've all pointed fingers at some one or
some thing for our lot in life. But sooner or later, if we are to cross
that bridge to mastery of Self and reunion with the God of our being,
we have to wake up to who's really been calling the shots. It's not
them from past or present and never has been.

Through these pages, I hope you will come to see this is not a
world of victimization, that you are not a little character being
moved around by circumstances out of your control. Rather, you are
a divine being endowed with the power to create in this lifetime however you wish to create. You are very much in control of your own
life. You, and you alone, control the power that can clear your path.
Indeed, you are the light at your feet.

THE WONDERFUL WORLD OF PROBLEMS

Stop to think about it. How would you feel, who would your
friends be, how would you live, dress, walk, or speak if you had no

problems? How at peace would you be if you had no bills, or hadn't been sexually abused, or had a different job? How would you feel without hate for a parent, or with a different boss, or lifemate? In short, how would you act without your problems?

Responses to the "who's responsible" questions, along with everything else in our lives we perceive to be the result of fate—therefore impossible to change—are the self-created roadblocks we routinely identify as problems. But for all we anguish over our problems, the truth is, no matter how much we think life would improve by changing them, or being without them, to freely give our problems up is terrifying. Sound crazy? Oh no. *Problems give us our identity!*

At a women's step-study meeting one night, we had finished reading Step Three from the "Twelve and Twelve" and were well into a discussion on turning our will and our lives over to the care of God as we understood Him, a process I was struggling with at the time, along with a life that was in an uproar. Somebody picked up a phrase in the chapter implying that many problems besides alcohol have a tough time yielding to individual will. While that was hardly a sage observation, a know-it-all old-timer retorted that there are no such things as problems, just our attitude towards living.

That's the only time in my life I can ever remember having a sincere desire to kill. My world's collapsing around me, I've got my ten-year Program by the skin of my teeth, and this gal's trying to tell me there are no problems in life?! In fact, my collapsing world *was* my life. It was all I knew. It was my identity.

We think we are our problems! We think they're a part of us. Well, they're not, and that's why we begin with the "who's responsible" questions, to see that all those hurts, blames, and regrets are what we think we are, or what we think we have to be, when in truth they're nothing more than our own limited thinking born in victimhood. They are how we've created our identity, the image we present to the outside world.

Having problems is a chronic habit. We live for the fool things! Having any sort of limited thinking is a habit and as insidiously addictive as any of the reasons for which we came to the Program. Like our booze, or food, or facilitating when we were practicing, we give those problems priority in our lives. We live by them. We are them. And we manufacture them with the consistency of an assembly line to give us the identity we think we need to have.

Let's say, for instance, you're sacrificing your life for your daughter; that's a limitation (limited thinking based in victimhood) and a manufactured identity. Or you can't get ahead in life because of your lack of education, another limitation and manufactured identity. Or you only attract jerks for lovers, a limitation and manufactured identity.

Limited thinking in any sense does not bode well for happiness, except in the glory of the manufactured identity, the *who* of what we *think* we are. We've created those roles, and we're going to hang on to them, come hell or high water.

Problems come into being through doubt in our real selves. Put another way, because we have no faith in the reality of what we really are, we've had to create identity shells. Out of feelings of worthlessness, or fear of nothingness, we manufacture identities to bring meaning to a life without apparent purpose, a life without an understanding of its own reality. Problems give us that purpose. Problems give us our imagined reality.

Look at how we live with problems. Our thoughts are consumed by them. Our world revolves around them. We plan with them, around them, and for them. We talk about them, go to psychiatrists over them, suffer silently with them, and spend endless hours totally immersed in them.

What would we be without our problems? They're so bloody dear to us that in the unlikely event one might get solved, instead of being grateful, we run right out and find another one, right now. And if it's not banging at our door, we go and borrow someone else's!

Living life at the mercy of our problems is living life as a victim.

T'WASN'T MY FAULT

Problems and blame go hand in hand. Who are you pointing a finger at for causing anything from a bad mood to your "lot in life"?

"If my son would only keep in touch, I wouldn't feel so unappreciated." "If my boss would recognize my talents, I would get a raise." "If the garage wasn't so small, I could get a new car." "If I had a love in my life, I wouldn't feel so lonely." "If I hadn't fallen into a river and swallowed a frog, I wouldn't be so afraid to sing."

We view problems through the eyes of blame as our excuses for not really living. The crux of this dilemma is that, in a constant state of blame, we have no need to take responsibility for our lives. Not only do we give up responsibility by placing blame outside ourselves, but we also give up choices. Ouch! And then, without choices, we've given up control. We've given our power to the problem, the person, or the event we blame. And considering there's hardly an area of our lives untouched by our perceived problems, that's one whale of a lot of power we've needlessly thrown away.

Blame doesn't mean who was right or wrong in the fender-bender at the intersection. Blame is that insidious thing with which we blackwash our entire world. We blame the rain for spotting our suit, the season for our "down" mood, our former addiction for our trouble with honesty, the government for poor education, or the crabgrass for a bad back. We eat, breathe, sleep, and play tennis in a world of unending blame. If you think you've stopped blaming since coming to the Program, you might take another look!

Interestingly, we started talking about problems and migrated right into blame. Of course! That's the safest and most reliable way to stay in the problem. Want to be sure you always have problems? Easy. Just keep up the blame! Problems and blame. They feed on each other. You can't have one without the other.

We've always looked outside ourselves to find reasons for why we are the way we are, feel the way we feel, or why our lives are going the way they're going. "S'not my fault that happened." "S'not my fault I'm this way." Or, here's the best one, "It was God's will, not mine."

Granted, many things in our past happened as a result of unconscious thought, families we don't remember asking for, sexual abuse, bodies we don't like, or any other quirks of so-called bad luck. But whether the circumstances came as a result of conscious thought or not, as long as we hold our past responsible for our fate today, we remain chained to a life without choices. We are living a life as a victim.

The Blame Game

OK now, let's define victim. Frankly, there are few among us who won't identify. To begin with, being a victim means existing in a world of helplessness, a world of looking to others to make us feel better, of pointing fingers at who did it to us. Right off the bat we have that sense of powerlessness, of being out of control. So the number one rule of living life as a victim is to eliminate the process called joy, for when we give our power away, joy goes with it.

Being a victim means routinely taking no responsibility for our own feelings. It means placing the cause of our feelings *out there*, assigning to others the myriad of reasons for our countless emotions and reactions. To a victim, almost all of life's circumstances have been absolutely unrequested and have been directly responsible for all unhappiness and failures.

Another major clue to being a victim is how much we stay hooked to the past, whether that past is five minutes or five decades ago. Stop to think about it. How can you hold a focus on events of yesterday and expect to have joy in your life today? You can't, because your point of power, or joy, is always in the now. The moment you give your power away to anything (people, places, or things), no matter how inconsequential, you move away from the now. You become a victim of circumstance, because once your power goes, your joy goes with it. Indeed, victimhood and joy simply cannot exist together.

Through all of our struggles, problems, and sacrifices we've been living the rules of the Blame Game. First comes a circumstance we don't like, then comes the blame, then comes the problem as a result of the blame, then we blame the problem for the unhappiness which came from the blame in the first place. Anyone for Ping-Pong? It's a dizzy, unhappy game we've chosen (yes, chosen!) to play all our lives, primarily because no one ever told us we didn't have to follow those rules.

Now, there's nothing either right or wrong about this; it just is. Where we go from here is to change it, a simple task once we see what we've been doing.

Remember, it's the separation from the real you, the God of your being, that's created the victim role. The moment you realize that, and accept it, you've started to live as a Master.

LIFE AS A MASTER

Life as a Master is only a thought away. It's coming to that place of knowing you do what you do, think the way you think, and feel the way you feel because you want to out of choice instead of helplessness.

As a Master, you stop giving your power away to the world. You allow, no longer playing into life's little dramas, understanding what's going on, without judgment. You take absolute control of your thoughts, fully understanding how your thoughts create your reality. You act differently and feel differently by choice. You live happily in the midst of what you know you have created yourself. Blame is not part of your world. As Master, you are in control.

If friends turn away from this new you (as they may do), you still love who and what you are. You appreciate that they are expressing at their level of understanding, and you allow their expression without judgment. You begin to live as you were created to live, with vibrancy, vitality, and fullness; in other words, happily.

As Master, you know you choose and create every circumstance in your life, big and small. (If you find that hard to swallow right now, stay with it; the reasons will soon unfold.) And if those circumstances were fear-based, you learn you created them deliberately for the experience of the emotion, and that now it's high time (and quite possible) to create new experiences without the old fears.

Perhaps most important, as Master you understand the divinity within you which endowed you with the power to create whatever your heart desires. You focus on what brings you joy and move on to it without regret.

There's no more shoulder-shrugging cop-out to God's will, or fate, or luck. Hand in hand with your own divinity, you know for sure who's calling the shots.

Who among us hasn't lived with uncertainty, unsure of decisions we've made or are making? That uncertainty (or fear) no longer exists when living life as a Master, because you base your decisions on what brings you joy, not selfishly through fear but with the deep inner security of your own divine love.

As a Master, you'll ask yourself at every turn, "For the love of whom am I doing this?" And there will be no uncertainty in your decisions. From depths of self-love, you'll always know what steps to take.

What is it, then, that changes your life so completely, so dramatically, from victim to Master? It's the confidence that comes from knowing who and what you really are. "If you want what we have, and are willing to go to any lengths to get it . . . ," don't let anything stand in your way. No matter what you have to let go of to get there, go for it. By God, go for it!

CROSSING THE BRIDGE

Something wonderful happens when you make the decision to cross the Bridge to Mastery. It's like being introduced to yourself for the first time. You know you're going for the Light within, and the awareness comes that, by God, you really are a lot more than you ever gave yourself credit for being. You're waking up, remembering bit by bit your real Self, remembering your divinity.

This is not a world of victimization. Whether we know it or not (or like it), we really are in control of our own lives. Up to now, we've let life splatter all over the place without much direction, thinking the struggle was normal, maybe even thinking it was happiness. We've been living life on this side of the bridge with little or no awareness of how we really do control every waking minute of every day.

By reaching out (or in) to your own power, you've taken the first step over the bridge. If you make the decision to go for it, or even to just test it out, you'll begin to experience a sense of excitement that automatically spills over into every area of your life.

Even the most mundane things take on a new glimmer of purpose until one day you find yourself wanting to literally race across the bridge rather than crawl. It's then you know some joyful voice inside is cheering, "You've got it, you've got it, keep going, you've really got it!"

Let it come. Step out of your own way and trust that inner voice. Fan your desire for more—more knowledge, more awareness, more awakening. Know with everything in you, there is nothing ahead that can keep you from your right to happiness and fulfillment. That Master of yours is right inside, pounding to be let out. Let it come, let it come, let it come!

A long time ago we each made a choice to deny the God within us, and up cropped separation, aloneness, blame, problems, and fear, the conflicts we've been struggling with ever since we were tiny tots. So it was with our parents, and their parents, and their parents, all from an understandable, perhaps even excusable, lack of knowledge.

But times are different now. A fresh new breeze is sweeping the planet. It's the wake-up call to remembrance, the call from deep within that beckons, "Cross the bridge, old friend, and come Home!"

CHAPTER 3

The Subconscious:
Master Controller

That hunger whirling around inside us wants to take hold and blast us off to somewhere. It wants to transform us from insecure to secure, from lonely to content, from bored to fulfilled, and from numb to alive. It's beckoning, pressing, pushing. And we say, "Hey, fine, I'm ready to go. But where? And how?"

Granted, we're open to the possibility that the something more we seek may be a stronger "conscious contact with God *as we understood Him,*"? but what does this really mean? And where do we start? The magic key that swings wide the doors to a life of all we've ever dreamed is thought, the very stuff of which we're made.

Most of us, at one time or another, have studied something about thought. We learned, for instance, we operate with a conscious and a subconscious mind. We have presumed, and been taught, that thought emanates from the brain. We've been taught what we think about is important and could possibly make a difference in our lives. But the idea that "thought" and God are one gets

a bit far-out, and has probably not been a major factor in our learning or seeking. Now, however, thought is going to play the starring
role.

The journey into thought is the journey into Self; the journey
into Self is the journey into God. The journey into God is the journey into Mind; the journey into Mind, the Supreme Intelligence, the
Creator and supportive element of all life, is the remembrance of
what we are. So we're going to do some serious thinking about
thought, for it's the stuff from which everything is created and without which nothing would exist, including us.

Thought is the Life Force, the Isness of the omniverse which
loves all that it is, and through that wondrous love allows all life to
be. And it is also the most remarkably misunderstood, misdirected,
misjudged, misused, abused, and ignored power in our world.

OUR GIANT MAGNET

Can you think back to a time when something exciting was in
the offing, but you just kept thinking to yourself, "Oh, that's never
going to happen," and it didn't? Can you remember when you
absolutely knew something would work, and it did? Or can you bring
to mind a deep belief you hold about your past you just know affects
your whole world?

What's in operation here is the subconscious, a portion of the
mind with which most of us are only moderately familiar. We've had
little notion about the extent of its involvement and power in our
lives.

Seeing ourselves as victims of circumstances, for instance, or as
a perceived success or failure, is a view which comes straight from

the subconscious. Our moods, reactions to people, places, and things, our self-image, and self-worth are all the result of silent thinking taking place in subconscious mind. In fact, just about everything we do or ever have done has been a result of what we've allowed to be programmed into our subconscious.

Somewhere along the way in our lives we picked up this habit of believing that so-and-so or such-and-such was responsible for whatever was going on in our world. No one ever told us that as long as we continued to look outside ourselves for reasons and answers our lives would be out of control. Actually, if you want to get right down to it, we never knew we were not in control.

The true director of this mayhem has been a subterranean powerhouse of stagnant, old beliefs buried beneath our conscious reality. So powerful are the magnetic properties of these hidden thoughts, the greatest span of our lives has been ruled by them.

Thoughts are things with an aliveness all of their own. They are little electromagnetic collectors of energy which eventually cause people, events, or circumstances to appear in our physical reality.

The challenge is, these little "things" have slipped into our subconscious as beliefs which we've long since forgotten about, and they've been wreaking havoc with our lives ever since. They have overridden wishes, dreams, and hopes, and have pre-programmed our lives as infallibly as the most brilliantly devised computer software package on the market today.

Since we've been unaware of this old programming, whenever our lives didn't suit us, we did what we were trained to do . . . place blame outside ourselves. *They* caused this, or *that's* what did it, when in fact it was usually the transmission of those subconscious thoughts, electromagnetically drawing unwanted and repetitious circumstances into our frustrated lives. *Their* fault? No. Our thoughts? You bet your life!

How do you think your tomorrows get made? From every thought you have today! And every thought you had yesterday. And most of these thoughts designing your todays and tomorrows are coming from that subterranean transmitter, your subconscious.

Talk about being held prisoner! (Well, we weren't, but let's do.) We're absolutely imprisoned by the beliefs we've stored in our sub-conscious over the years. If you've ever wanted an explanation for why your life is the way it is, that's it!

Just look at the questionable quality of stuff we store away: beliefs about the human race, the opposite sex, our own sex, sex itself, authority figures, self-worth, families, love, happiness, fears, should's and shouldn'ts. Like a giant magnet, our subconscious is controlling our world with these silent thoughts, day in and day out.

Whether we're aware of our beliefs or not, whether they are hid-den from our conscious minds or not, *we experience as we believe.* The ups, the downs, the so-called positive and negative events of our lives, are all a product of what we—not any one else—hold to be true. We experience as we believe! What a mighty truth! To learn to command that power—a power so strong it could move moun-tains—is the longing of our soul. It's what *this* trip is all about.

The good news is we *can* take control. The very same power which has enslaved us for most of our lives can be turned around to bring us more incredible freedom and power than we ever dared imagine; a life without fear, without doubt or pain; a life of fulfill-ment, with direction and purpose. Pie in the sky? Not by a long shot. We've carried this awesome power within us since the day we were born. Now it's time we learn to use it.

WHAT IS SUBCONSCIOUS MIND?

Think of an iceberg. The small segment we see jutting from the water is like our conscious mind, a mere fraction of the whole. What lies beneath the surface is the subconscious, mammoth, powerful, and very well hidden.

That hidden power represents anywhere from seventy percent to ninety percent of the whole. In other words, our *conscious* mind is only ten percent to thirty percent activated, with the remainder underground working day and night, without our conscious awareness.

Consciousness, whether the tip of the iceberg or the power below, is all energy. It controls the workings of our atoms, regulating all of our cellular activity. Our body is consciousness. Space is consciousness. In fact, *everything* is consciousness. And energy, in turn, is created from the use of consciousness.

Within the body, consciousness splits into three operational parts: (1) the inner self, or ego, that aspect that makes us think we are what we are; (2) the body consciousness that keeps us physically together and functioning even when we're "gone," as in sleep or other states of unconsciousness; and (3) the consciousness we know which picks up and emanates thought. Put them all together; they spell You. And it's all energy, pure, explosive, magnetic, limitless energy.

We find the subconscious in the first of the three, the inner self, doing what it's told to do, when it's told to do it, and never, but *never*, disobeying those orders until it receives new ones. That's its job!

The operation of our subconscious is the operation of our very lives. Everything we do, the way we act, the way we dress, our lack or abundance, people we gather about us, they all come from the programming of our subconscious mind. We're seemingly helpless in the presence of its force. But hear ye, hear ye; we're helpless only to the degree that we allow it to continue ungoverned!

Since we were little tykes, our subconscious has absorbed and swallowed statements and emotions into its permanent storage as beliefs. It's our emotional governing body. It's taken orders from our consciousness (intentionally or not), from our imagination, from people around us, and obediently sent back the responses which run our lives, whether we like them or not.

For all the power this thing has, though, it's never had a mind of its own. It can't analyze, can't figure anything out for itself, has no power of choice or logic, yet directs our daily lives by offering us *programmed reactions* to any given situation.

So here you are living inside this superpower called Mind (we don't *have* a mind, we *are* mind), apparently reduced to helpless jelly in the presence of this mighty force called the subconscious. You have only to change what's held there, and you're in control. You change your life forever.

THE POWER OF THE SUBCONSCIOUS

People tend to think of the subconscious as some dark store-house of horrors. It's not. It's just a garage filled with litter that needs cleaning out. So one day we start to sort it through and hold a garage sale. Bit by bit we weed through the old junk, deciding what to toss and what to keep. The obsolete stuff we've been hoarding for way too long needs to go, and it will, the moment we make the decision to let go of it and reprogram.

Reprogramming, though, doesn't happen from wishful thinking or even red-faced determination. The subconscious can't be fooled. If you don't believe the new material you're sending down, it will always act from old programming, and your attempt at self-deception will keep you right in the middle of good, old-fashioned self-sabotage. It's by working from your core with your Inner Being that you bring about the believability in your new programming (new beliefs), and the subconscious reacts accordingly.

Several years ago, when I had about fifteen years on the Program along with a supposedly sound spiritual base, I was selling ranch lands in central California. These were big pieces of property with big prices and deliciously big commissions. The first self-sabotage came on a beautiful and unique piece fronting the spectacular coastline at Big Sur. My Oklahoma clients loved the property, and my sellers were flabbergasted that I had found buyers so quickly.

The commission was to be around $110,000, which in the late seventies was a sizable amount, but I couldn't shake the gnawing fear that it was all just too good to be true. Nonetheless, both buyer and seller eagerly signed the escrow papers. The commission seemed assured as closing day approached. And the closer it got, the more fearful I became.

Sure enough, on the day it was to close, the thing fell irreparably apart! The why's and how's are immaterial, but at the time I simply chalked it up to bad luck, operating straight from victimhood.

A few months later I sold a magnificent three-hundred-acre ranch right in front of our house. Lush, green fields with views of forever swept down to the ocean. A major southern California developer had gone over the ranch with a fine-tooth comb and agreed it was just what he wanted. Again I was a "knightess" in shining armor to owners who had been trying to sell this property for almost five years. There I was with sale papers ready to sign in less than three months of taking the listing. Once again, everybody signed.

Once again, both parties were delighted. Once again, I was looking at a huge commission, this time for $160,000! And once again, I was in a state of near panic.

One day after the signing of the papers by both parties, who had each worked diligently to incorporate verbiage into the contract making any breakdown impossible, it fell apart . . . for good. And again I chalked it up to bad luck.

That happened only once more before I got out of that end of the business. This time the commission was $180,000 plus a one-sixteenth interest in the business, a gold mine of grape production. My client was ecstatic over the property I'd found for him. He'd been looking, to no avail, for a year and a half with a host of brokers. We were simply waiting for a redo on the title report before closing.

Outwardly, I was certain all was well, but my insides were again in turmoil. I tried to "turn it over" but found myself needing to be in absolute control to subdue the fear. The report came. My buyer found a tiny title variance not big enough to cause more than a mild "Oh really? No problem!" type of comment. He backed out.

Bad luck? Tough breaks? Not at all. Two things were at work here which shot those three commissions down with precision aim. The first was my subconscious programming regarding my inability to trust myself. It didn't matter how much I thought I was turning it over to my Higher Power. Way down inside, where I had no conscious knowledge of its existence, was a set of beliefs which said, "But you don't trust it to happen because it's all controlled by you, and you don't trust *you!*" To go against this programming would have been utterly impossible from a vantage of wishful thinking.

The second factor was what my thoughts were sending out . . . fear, buckets of fear that the transactions would not go through. I was being ruled by my own mistrust of myself, sending out thoughts so powerful they literally fanned the buyer's most insignificant doubts. He changed his mind. The deal was off. I had no trust in my Higher Power. It was all ego-control, pure self-will run riot without an ounce of God-power behind it. I was running on the same old program, setting myself up for failure time after painful time.

No matter what our conscious desire may be (and I certainly had a conscious desire to have those commissions!), we are governed and limited by whatever beliefs are stored in our subconscious.

COLLISION COURSE

By and large, we're operating on material programmed into the subconscious during roughly the first twelve years of life. Startling? Yes, considering the amount of input, but the pattern *is* reversible. It's simply a matter of tuning into everything being broadcast from our hidden transmitter, all that stuff in the garage waiting to be cleaned out.

Take, for example, the self-image which comes from the subconscious. It tells us if we are to be prosperous or struggling, confident or shy, attractive or unattractive, happy or bored. If the programming says we're not good enough, we aren't. If it tells us we can't hold on to a life partner, we don't.

Or take habits. They're programmed like automatic pilots. There you are in your little airplane, cruising along, enjoying the scenery. You decide you'd like to relax and enjoy the view, so you put your plane on automatic. Ah, perfect. Now you can lean back and enjoy the sights. Of course your autopilot doesn't stop to reason that you might have set it improperly. It just steers you on . . . straight into the side of a mountain.

The same is true of all subconscious beliefs, old or new. They're just more autopilot programs, locking us solidly into a life course without the slightest awareness or concern they may be heading us straight for disaster.

ELEPHANTS AND US

Do you remember the story of the six-thousand-pound elephant in the circus who never tried to get away from the thin rope which tethered him to a small wooden stake? There he was, this massive chunk of power who could have broken the rope or pulled up the stake in a twinkling of an eye. So why didn't he? When he was a baby, his masters put a heavy chain around his foot and attached it to a strong metal stake cemented deep into the ground. Only an eighteen-wheeler could have pulled it up. The little elephant learned to believe he couldn't escape. He was a prisoner of his subconscious beliefs. No matter what opportunity came his way for escape, he would always be tethered by that limited belief.

Sometimes we're aware of our thoughts which can turn to beliefs (or already have), sometimes we're not. To make this point, a group I was working with engaged in a rather arduous experiment. For six hours straight, everyone sat with pencil and paper writing down whatever thoughts jumped into their heads with the proviso there be no editing. "This is a dumb experiment. My back aches. I forgot to call my sister. God, I left the back porch light on. Guess Jerry will be late again tonight as usual. Sure would be great being married to someone who cares enough to come home on time. Maybe he's got a girlfriend. I don't like the girl sitting next to me. Dumb thing to say, I don't even know her. Wonder why her husband likes her. I bet her kids are ugly monsters. . . ."

It was a tough six hours, vividly pointing out the plethora of negative trivia we allow to run through our minds, trivia we accept as valid and therefore record permanently in our subconscious programming.

You know the computer saying, "Garbage in, garbage out." Well, negative trivia and outdated beliefs from past or present are the kind of "garbage in" that's been running our lives. And even innocent, passing thoughts such as we poured out in those six hours are recorded as beliefs, stored for recall at any moment to manipulate our world.

OUR WORLD OF CAUSE AND EFFECT

Every thought we accept as valid is a cause for some type of effect in our life. The thought is the *cause*—the thing that's going to make something happen—and the happening, as a result of the thought, is the *effect*. Or, put another way, every unrecognized thought stored in your subconscious is a *cause* for some *effect* or circumstance in your life. That's how the subconscious maintains control over our world.

"Now wait just a darn minute," you say. "Are you trying to tell me my thinking is causing my wife to be drunk every night when I get home? Or because of the way I think, my mother-in-law is coming here to live? Or it's my thoughts that are preventing me from finding the kind of work I want? Come on! Get real!"

If your subconscious is programmed with a need to control (thoughts stemming from fear), that could be why you're living with a drunk, to have someone to control. If you have an unrecognized dislike of authority figures, you may unknowingly manipulate your mother-in-law's arrival as a means to more safely work out some of those hidden aggressions. Or, if you've been programmed to believe you are in any way *less than*, finding the kind of job you want could be extremely tough.

These are simple examples of old, programmed thoughts, the causes, producing present-day circumstances, the effects. But new thinking is equally powerful in causing effects.

For example, I used to go around telling everyone what a jerk I was for doing such-and-such. It seemed to improve my image by demeaning myself so grandly. Little did I know my subconscious was taking me literally, classifying *jerk* in the same file as all the other times I had referred to myself as *less than*, joking or not. Believe me, that kind of programming plays havoc with people's ability to manifest anything but junk in their lives. I don't kid around with words anymore!

Indeed, the subconscious takes for granted we know what we're doing, obediently accepting as truth whatever we send it in spoken words or silent thoughts. We send it the causes (thoughts), and it provides the effects (reactions or circumstances).

GETTING NEW EFFECTS

Here's a good example of changing cause and effect. A friend of mine, whom I'll call Bob, was sexually abused as a child by his uncle. He believed this to be the reason for his impotence and emotionalized that belief as a fact. The actual act of abuse, of course, could not directly or physically cause such a reaction, but it had become Bob's truth! The habit of being impotent was solidified.

To change the effect (i.e., being impotent), Bob knew he had to change what his subconscious believed. He also knew he had to put an intense emotional charge behind the desired new programming, or it would have no effect in erasing the old.

So he called on his Higher Power to help create a new belief. The subconscious said, "Aha! Strong new program coming down on uncle." Bob's "problem" was being overridden with a new emotional belief and rapidly disappeared. He had shredded his blame file headed "Uncle's Fault" and replaced it with "It's not fact; it's only my perception, which I now choose to change."

"Uncle" was never the enemy, just Bob's thoughts about uncle. What other people may have done in our life is inconsequential. They only created the event, but we created the blame, or belief, around the event to be the cause of our current effects. Change the worn-out belief with new thinking, and you change your life.

A New Perception

We dream of a life without our "if only's," of different beginnings, of different circumstances. We wish it could be "this way" and wonder why it's not. We want the new, but hesitate to get rid of the old because we're so comfortable with the predictability. We seek escape through "geographical cures," new clothes, or new relationships, when in fact the only change that was ever permanent was a permanent change of thought.

We begin to alter the framework of our lives by realizing we were the ones who framed it. So we take the first steps to growth by accessing our lives and seeing a need for change. Then we allow ourselves the grace and humbleness to let go. The changes begin.

Change is a time when the limitations of old programming are torn away to make room for the new. Change raises us to a new level of thought, a new attitude, a new perception. Change is letting go completely of old ideas, and consciously reprogramming the subconscious with the new. Change is loving ourselves enough to release what inhibits our happiness and joy.

People did not shape our world; we did! Circumstances did not shape our lives; we did! So we go to our Source within and ask for help with removing old beliefs which no longer serve us. We don't even have to know what they all are; we just release them.

And then we ask for help in reprogramming. A different kind of energy is drawn to us, bringing new experiences to match the new beliefs. The life we once thought to be filled with smashed hopes takes on a shimmering new look. Wishes turn to desire; desire works with divine high-frequency energy and turns to reality. We're taking control of our life, directing it through our own divinity.

CHAPTER 4

OUR POWER WITHIN

In the Big Book of Alcoholics Anonymous, under the chapter to the agnostics, we find, "deep down in every man, woman, and child is the fundamental idea of God. It may be obscured by calamity, by pomp, by worship of other things, but in some form or other it is there." And, "We found the Great Reality deep down within us. In the last analysis it is only there that He may be found" (p.55).

Within the parameters of our Program we've established some sort of contact with a Higher Power. If we've always believed in God, perhaps that Higher Power is our God of old, separate from ourselves, but a power nonetheless from which we can draw. We turn to it for help in crisis, or even ask for comfort with the day-to-day broken shoelaces.

Perhaps our Higher Power, if not God, is the group, or a tree, or a sponsor. Indeed, Higher Powers of every description have been keeping Twelve-Steppers sober, clean, smokeless, non-dependent, thin, or out of Vegas for decades.

But there's always been this strange separation. For some reason, Higher Powers got placed *out there*, making *conscious contact* an effort, if not a struggle. While our Higher Power has been a mysterious wonder which most of us do ultimately come to believe in, and which we're fairly sure works if called upon, we rarely feel any sort of identification with it, except intellectually. We almost always think it's greater than we are, and someplace other than within us.

In truth, Higher Powers have come and gone in our lives like so much gas in our car. Empty? Fill it up. Since the Program began, well-meaning sponsors have been unwittingly perpetrating this concept. "No, honey," they say to their newcomers, "your Higher Power didn't leave you; you left your Higher Power." The separation, always the separation.

From childhood, most of us have looked to a source outside ourselves to fill that haunting void. We've sought to fill the emptiness with our addictions, with our relationships, and with our Higher Power. For the most part, only in times of dire need have we sincerely attempted to make conscious contact.

Thankfully, we did come to believe that a power greater than ourselves could restore us to sanity, or we might not have made it. Now we need to shift our focus and realize the power we're talking about is not greater than ourselves; *it is what we are!*

In a sense, one could say the power is indeed greater than our ego-selves. But nonetheless, this power is right within us. Always has been, always will be. And it's true no human power removed our addiction, because human power is ego power. So what happened? How did we get clean?

We had an urgent, driving need to change. When we called for help from our Higher Power, all universal forces—the forces of heaven which are *without*, as well as the force of our Inner Being *within*—united to magnetically draw new realities into our world.

With the help of our Inner Being (our Higher Power), we were sending powerful new orders to the subconscious. Because we knew it would work, we placed no blame on anyone and took full responsibility for our thoughts. It worked. When we allowed our Higher Power to take over, it worked.

Think back to the intense desire that brought you to the Program. It worked because the very intensity of that desire caused your Inner Being to fan it into a flame. You wanted change; you demanded it! There was nothing willy-nilly about your desire, and your subconscious got the message, loud and clear. You were operating on pure God-power, the secret key to changing the subconscious.

THE SECRET KEY

As we begin to learn the true nature of our power within in terms of composition, energy, purpose, and capabilities, we begin to ease into a shift of focus. Up to now, we've always turned a problem over, sending it off outside ourselves, giving up any responsibility for the results. Now we learn how to call on that vast inner power to interact with our subconscious mind. We learn that by consciously working with our Inner Being we can make whatever permanent changes we desire.

Sure, we still "leave the results to God," *but responsibility for those results is ours by the very nature of our consciously focused thought.* The consequences are no longer the responsibility of something out there.

In our new way of thinking, we see the tri-fold combination of our conscious, subconscious, and Inner Being all reacting with the energy of the universe to draw to us our soul's desire. That's leaving the results to God!

You do the reprogramming; you call on the power within as well as without (for they are one); with full realization you are now taking control of your life's design.

Knowing the process has begun, you step out of the way, let your subconscious go to work, and leave the production details—not the results—to the universe powers within and without, as one. Never mind how it's all going to work; just focus on the results, get out of the way, and let it all happen.

Something wonderful is stirring now. You learn to trust implicitly the wisdom of your subconscious mind and its ability to work for you because you know its orders have consciously come from the Highest Source. And you're operating from a new base of trust that your subconscious will respond accordingly.

Once orders have been given, backed by the power of your Inner Being, a kind of calm, all-pervading knowing fills your world. (I think they call it serenity.) No matter what chaos is being wrought on the outside, you know without any question how to handle it from the inside. *You're in control.* Powerless over your addiction, yes, because your addiction comes from your ego-self; but powerless over your life, no, for now the power of the universe is living through you. With this awareness realized, you are at last in control.

Without question, the strength of our Inner Being is the key to unlocking the vast powers of our subconscious. That strength is what we are. It stands ready to ignite our world, not tomorrow or in some hazy unidentifiable future, but right now. All we have to do is say, "Yeah! I'm ready!"

IN THE FLOW

Before long, you'll be able to tell the difference between the two wills, ego-will and God-will. One driver will continue to run you on bumpy roads, giving you the same old cuts and bruises, while the other will run you along smooth highways where everything feels right and even. That's being in the flow. The flow is the Life Force. The flow is God. The flow is your own energy. The flow is what you are.

One of the best examples of being in the flow is having "an attitude of gratitude." That's no laughing matter with your subconscious, for when that gratitude is sincerely felt, your Inner Being absolutely takes over and downright insists that your subconscious shut up and listen to the new programming. It will. If you were to maintain an attitude of gratitude on a regular basis while thoroughly reprogramming your subconscious, you'd be attracting so much abundance, you'd have to hire a crew to help you handle it all. That's being in the flow.

Just working with your Inner Being in *any* way automatically puts you in the flow. It'll arrange anything for you with absolutely no effort on your part, except the effort of consciously directing your thoughts.

When you're in the flow, the stones on your path are no longer insurmountable boulders but merely items to be acknowledged, used as lessons, then stepped over. Difficulties melt away before they have a chance to materialize. Sizable promises, yes, but I know them to be true. They've all happened to me.

WE CAME; WE CAME TO; WE CAME TO REMEMBER

Most of us have no idea what we're all about. Surely I had no idea of the nature of my reality. I lived in my secure little box, totally addicted to my graduate degree in victimhood, and living for my precious ego-identity.

With great diligence I sought my Higher Power on a regularly irregular basis which seemed to go in cycles. One year the Eleventh Step[1] and I would be inseparable, and the next I'd get lazy and end up wondering why my world seemed so topsy-turvy. One year I'd be into an abundance of inventories to take my spiritual temperature, and the next ignoring almost anything having to do with spirituality.

From all outward appearances, I really had it together: my own business, a perfect relationship, a good Program, many "babies," a fair amount of speaking at meetings, some institutional work, and always showing up at our local conventions. I thought I had all I could ever want except more money, which was forever in excruciatingly short supply.

But underlying all of the outpicturing was a dis-ease, a deep hurting I could never put my finger on. Thanks to the Program, my list of "if only's" was getting shorter each year, but the blame I placed on myself for not producing more dollars was crushing. And any blame I placed on my relationship, for anything, I hid from myself in deep denial.

My poor subconscious had little rest from cranking out the old programming. Day after day I'd see all my shortcomings holding me back. Bad luck seemed to surround me in business, and it was no small effort to keep up the appearance of the "got-it-together kid," when on the inside I was bleeding nails.

---

[1] The Eleventh Step of Alcoholics Anonymous: "Sought through prayer and meditation to improve our conscious contact with God *as we understood Him*, praying only for knowledge of His will for us, and the power to carry that out" (p. 59).

The insidious thing about this kind of thinking is, like any addiction, it grows. My need for a more secure sandbox in which to maintain my image was growing rapidly. And the stronger I allowed my image to grow, the less able I seemed to be to work with my Higher Power.

The dollar sabotages became more frequent, and I was beginning to feel as if I existed solely by the grace of Crazy Glue which was also helping to keep the smile stuck on my face. The right words were coming out at meetings, but my insides were in turmoil. It was no longing. It was a noticeable scream for help, but help from what, I had no idea. Where was I going? Who was I? Where was my Higher Power? There had to be more than this!

When my sixteen-year relationship crumbled, I flew into a million pieces, twenty-three years of sobriety notwithstanding. All the old programming in my subconscious came roaring to the fore. My identity was shattered. There was nothing to hang on to. I could no longer blame my significant other for my pain and discomfort. Where could I turn? My Higher Power had gone for a vacation to the Milky Way. My good old subconscious was saying, "You asked for this," while my head was saying, "How could this possibly happen to me? Look at what a wonderful person I've been in this relationship."

In every argument I had with myself, the winner was always my subconscious, though I didn't know this at the time. It didn't give a damn about my pain and just kept calling the shots, calling forth the events in my daily life that I was positive I didn't want.

Though I had not the slightest idea to whom or what I was sending my pleas for help—Higher Power or anything else—it didn't matter to me as long as Something heard and answered. My pleas were unending and, before long, were bringing changes in my life.

An Adult Children of Alcoholics workshop *just happened* to open up and began the turnaround by giving an enormous boost to my self-esteem. New people *just happened* to come into my life. New events, new meetings, new opportunities, strangers recommending life-changing books. I was drawing a new world to me, and was somewhat unsure what to make of it all.

Then came the major turnaround. With timid and somewhat fearful steps, I took a week's vacation by myself and for seven magnificent days looked into the glassy reflections of a mountain lake in California's High Sierra. The pain of the breakup was still with me, holding the terrible rawness of only three months. Oh, that awful pain!

For lack of anything else better to do, I had taken with me a new little book about using the powers of the mind. It told how, with the help of the All In All, we can reprogram our subconscious to rid our lives of suffering, no matter how intense (Murphy 1980).

The desire within me now for a closer contact with my Higher Power was overwhelming. Sitting beside the still, midnight-blue waters and allowing the glitter from the sun's backlighting to play twinkles on my body and spirit, I once again spoke an earnest plea to my God as I understood Him, which said simply, "Help me. Oh, dear God, please help me know what to do."

One of the affirmations in the book kept showing up again and again, and I realized I could reshape it to my own needs and truly believe it. "My love is gone, and I am at peace." The first part was obviously true, so I had no trouble with that. The second part was true only because of my abiding love of lakes. No matter, it was true, I *was* at peace beside the deep quiet of the lake.

By the end of the week and after reciting that potent little affirmation thousands of times, the pain had lifted completely.

Completely! A new kind of full and beautiful love for the one with whom I had shared those sixteen years came into my being. Today we're the closest of friends.

"Bad days" became a thing of the past. I learned how to forgive myself. Yes, myself! But most important, I began the process of identifying what needed to be reprogrammed within me, calling forth the power of that-which-I-am to help with the process. I knew at long last I would be able to attract the kinds of experiences and circumstances which up to then had been only hopeless dreams.

Since God's work is never done, neither am I, but one thing is for sure. To paraphrase one of our favorite sayings from the Program, my best days in sobriety, prior to this new way of thinking and living, can't hold a candle to my worst days today. There is simply no comparison. The God that I am is in control (most of the time).

Above all, I no longer call forth my limitations ("I'm always broke," "I'm single," "It's their fault") to create my identity. I will simply not allow them in my life any longer. Instead, I call forth my unlimited potential, and out it pours.

I live on a little farm, doing what I want to do, when I want to do it. I have money and peace and friends and abundance and fun and gaiety and fulfillment of work. I know how to bring the things I want into my life and how to keep out those things I don't want. I'm happy; there's no other way to say it. I know what I am, where I'm going, and, for the most part, how to get there.

God and I are at One with each other, but it's not spiritual driveling. Sometimes it's pure bliss. Other times it's being in a state of allowing, allowing some fears to come up and pass through, or judgments to be experienced. They are, I do, and it's back again to energetic happiness.

Yes, I engage it daily, many times hourly, not because I have to *maintain*, but because the hunger inside of me is a long way from being satisfied. It just grows and grows, only this time I know what the hunger is and feed it with a passion of joy and tears and playfulness. My journey has become my new life, and I love every blessed second of it!

Each of us hit our respective "bottom" that got us to the Program. Now a new kind of "bottom" has come into our lives, not as terrifying, perhaps, but just as empty—if not more so. Mine was like that, and I bless it, for I know now that we've come to this life to explore, to have adventures, and to grow closer to the Light we are. We have not come here to have pain, anguish, guilt, and lack. Indeed, we are here to learn. And that yearning we've been experiencing is our soul trying to tell us it's time to begin the reprogramming. Now!

We no longer have to bump into the same obstacles over and over, or play the same old games. My God! Isn't that a revelation? The process of our waking up begins, the reprogramming begins, our soul hollers hallelujahs and, without missing a beat, life starts changing. *Cause* now begins to bring refreshing—and highly welcomed—*effects*.

When we first came to the Program, we were eager to learn, although we'd often intellectualize the new concepts to the point of absurdity. But how many times did our wise sponsors caution us to keep it simple? Uh-huh! How many times were we advised to get ourselves out of the way, or to "utilize, not analyze"? Uh-huh!

No difference here. Keep it simple. Keep yourself out of your way. Utilize, don't analyze, and watch your life change. *You will come to recognize your divinity,* and therein lies the answer to the search we've all been on for oh, so long.

We live in a loving universe with all manner of forces surrounding us to give assistance and support as we learn. We no longer need to deny that tremendous longing within, for we are the creative essence of God, creating what we've allowed to be programmed within us, learning to create our *own* truths and be in control. Once we locate that core, our Inner Being, the piece of God we are, we know we're not alone, and our world changes forever.

RECALLING THE SONG

Haven't you ever felt a kind of knowingness within, which understands why you're here? We each have that deep knowingness, our Inner Being, pressing for us to wake up and start the reprogramming, pressing us to begin this precious journey back to Self, the journey back to God, the journey back to what we are.

No, we don't jump from first grade to graduate school in one session. The thrills on this journey come in stages as our subconscious begins to take in new "orders," and we gradually allow our Inner Being to take over the controls from our ego. Goodness knows, it's been waiting long enough to do just that.

Along the way, you may bump into circumstances that seem to be at total odds with this new path, things like a "bad" situation turning even worse for a while. That's OK. Relax and allow it all to unfold. Stay out of the "how to's."

You're going into an old, self-created darkness. As you learn to assume full responsibility for that darkness, lights will start to go on all over the place, and you'll see things very, very differently. Your whole perspective on life—your life—will change, whether you're looking at a blade of grass or a company proposal. Just allow the bumps, and know that they are temporary.

It's all a matter of accepting, accepting the power of the subconscious, which is part of our Inner Being, to manifest desirable experiences in our life. The walls of resistance do melt away. Now comes the real fun as you watch manifestations unfold in your life in ways you could never, ever begin to dream.

Actually, this journey is not unlike the one you've been on since coming to the Program, just a little deeper. Be gentle with yourself as you go forward into the unknown. Know you are safe. Know there is help all about you. Follow your heart and know that you know. If you want it, your new life will unfold.

Ask for understanding as you read these pages. Ask, ask, and ask again. This is probably very new territory. Be open. The more open your mind, the more those magnificent little awakenings will come which you'll find delicious beyond words. Yes, you *will* start to remember what you are, a little here, a little there, like an ancient song, long forgotten.

Listen for it. Go within and see how much you can remember. Perhaps you don't remember the whole melody, yet somehow you'd know if it were to come back to you, you'd weep at the remembrance of how dear the strains were to you in another time.

The process of remembering this song is our journey, a trip all heaven stands ready to help us with, once we put out the call and ask. We can be in the midst of anything, with the world apparently crumbling at our feet, and say, "Help me, teach me." Help will come. New ways to reprogram old thinking, new ideas, new situations. Help will come!

We are here to bring back into our awareness the understanding that we and our Source are One, and that by working with this unlimited power, we *can* reverse that old programming. Be open; let it unfold; try it on for size. It will happen if you want it to. These next steps into life are what you yourself have called forth.

CHAPTER 5

THOUGHT: OUR CONNECTION TO GOD

The best way to fill a room with light and fresh air is to raise the shades and open the windows. So it is with knowledge. We could work for ten eternities trying to shovel out the darkness of ignorance when all we have to do is step to the window and let in the light of knowledge.

So it is with the impressive topic of thought. In actuality, to understand thought is simply to understand what we are, a part of the Oneness of all energy everywhere. From that premise, we easily learn to use the powerful energy which thought creates to change our lives.

There are really only two basic elements to remember in understanding the nature of thought. First is that every one of our thoughts is a very alive thing with a life and power of its own. Second, and unquestionably the most important, is that each particum of thought we transmit *links magnetically* with identical energies to manipulate our daily lives!

So what are we? We're energy—pure God-energy—living in matter, which, too, is a form of energy. But because we generally perceive the body as our only reality, physical mass as opposed to dynamic energy, we miss out on almost everything true life has to offer.

The truth of the matter is the body is not what we are, thought is; thought, powered by various degrees of emotional energy. All that remains is remembering how to harness it.

A word of caution: please don't get caught up in the physics of this information. Just ride along to get the overview of what thought is, where it comes from, how we move it, what it does, and how it acts. Draw back the shades, open the windows, and have fun with this information; it's probably unlike anything you have ever read.

THE BRAIN AND THE MIND

Scientists are just beginning to piece together the mind-boggling implications behind their discoveries as to the nature of thought. Although the field is young, what's been uncovered is enormously exciting. Thoughts are in motion about us all the time, all thoughts great and small, every thought of everything that is known. By various electromagnetic means, we choose certain thoughts as they zip by, drawing them to us through the energy field that surrounds our body. At this point in our lives, however, we're still pulling in the same old thoughts over and over again with the specialities of the day being unworthiness, depression, fear, struggle, etc. These are known as "limited" thoughts.

To begin the study of thought, we look first to the brain. If you're like the vast majority of folks in this world, including most (but not all) scientists, you probably believe the mind and brain are

THOUGHT: OUR CONNECTION TO GOD

one. You also probably believe the brain is the birthplace of thought. Most modern medical theory, in fact, sticks to the belief that the main function of the brain is mind, which manifests ideas by forming those familiar patterns of electrochemical activity seen as electrical brain waves in the nerves of the cerebral cortex.

Actually, the brain is only the biochemical electrical switchboard which the mind uses as the link between our God within (our Inner Being) and the body it occupies. Mind and brain exist apart from one another yet operate together. So what is mind? Mind is consciousness, both aware consciousness and subconsciousness. Faithful old brain is what makes it work, because that brain of ours is actually one giant receiver!

Every split second of every day these billions upon billions of thought propellants bombard us in unending streams. They look something like straight-line rays of light. Magnetically charged, they travel at unmeasurable speeds through the energy field which surrounds our body and on into the brain.

What we know as consciousness is actually an endless flow of these countless little propellants that never ceases to surround us. Everywhere we are, everywhere we look, and everything we see is the result of conscious thought. Even deep space is deep thought, consciousness, in never-ending movement.

So the brain as the receiver of thought allows the propellants to enter from this consciousness flow, transforms them into an electrical current, amplifies them, then sends them through the central nervous system to every part of our body to be translated into an understanding of some sort. "What was that impulse? Oh, amusement? Gotcha. Thank you."

The catalyst that causes thought to propel itself into the brain is the powerful electromagnetic energy field which surrounds our bodies, that scientifically acknowledged (and often photographed) mass of energy also known as the auric field. With its powerful magnetism, this field attracts the charged thought propellants. But then it starts acting like a sieve, letting some in and keeping most out. The reason for this strange sorting-out process is that most of our brain is still asleep, unable to receive the ocean of unlimited thought which surrounds us. Here's how it works.

Our brains currently operate at only one-third capacity. (Russian scientists say as low as one-tenth.) That one-third is capable of receiving only the lower frequencies of limited thought, or what's known as "social consciousness" (fear, competition, anger, lack, survival, etc.). Higher-frequency thoughts, which are what we're missing most of the time, can only be received by that two-thirds portion of the brain still dormant. Getting that two-thirds operational is what this journey to our divinity is all about.

Want to know what Einstein knew? Want to know about the formation of the universe? Want to compose like Mozart? If our brains were totally open we could receive all thought flowing constantly about us, from the highest vibratory frequencies of the Christ/Buddha/Mohammed-type consciousness, to the understanding of Einstein's theories, to knowing how Scottie beams 'em up on *Star Trek*. But right now, even though our brains are equipped to receive the highest of frequencies, those lower frequencies of social-consciousness-limited-thinking are all that can get in.

So here we are, walking around inside this energy field (often called the spirit of our being) which is designed to pick up *all* frequencies of thought once the brain is fully opened. However, until we open it up more so that more of it is in use (and this is the key), the auric field can only pick up those lower frequencies on which the brain is currently operating. By the same token, the frequency the brain transmits depends upon how open it is at the time.

Still with me? Let's run it down this way: our first goal is to open the brain more, which will raise its frequency, which will automatically charge the energy field with the higher vibrations, which will enable the field to receive, and then transmit, the higher impulses of thought.

While the brain does not create thought (it accepts and transmits), it's the first place thought lands on its journey through the body. When a thought comes zooming in through the energy field, it goes directly to the brain, then zips to the cerebellum or the frontal lobes. That's where the first electrical impulses of thought end up and is what the medical community sees on the brain-wave printout from an EEG (electroencephalogram).

Science, of course, understands that the brain's neurons, those specialized cells of the nervous system which conduct impulses, generate their own electricity and that some of those neurons are tuned to fire only if they receive a certain number of impulses. They accept now that the cellular functions of our brains (and bodies) are controlled by actual DC (direct current) fields. And they're coming to understand that variations in that DC current correlate with every conscious or unconscious thought we have. So far, so good.

What's not so clearly understood, though, is that as the level of thought frequency increases (as when we concentrate on more expanded thought such as joy, love, life, oneness, energy, God, etc., rather than mundane, day-to-day, social-consciousness stuff), a greater hormone flow is produced throughout the body which in turn sparks the entire process of opening up the rest of the brain. And what creates this increased hormone flow is the pituitary gland, located between and at the base of the two frontal lobes, sort of right in the middle of the head. It's this wondrous little gland which opens the brain to receive the higher frequencies of greater thought.

THE JEWEL OF OUR BEING

The pituitary is about the size of a hazelnut, shaped like a little pear with its mouth at the narrow end. When thought comes into the brain, it hits the pituitary, which then secretes a hormone that flows through the brain into the pineal gland, another member of the endocrine system. The pineal, a tiny pinecone-shaped gland projecting down from the back of the brainstem, is the guy that's responsible for amplifying the thought frequencies when they're received so they can be dispatched throughout the body.

First, then, comes the thought propellant, which stimulates the pituitary, which activates the hormone flow from the pituitary into the pineal, which activates certain parts of the brain to receive the different frequencies of thought. Right now, of course, the mouth of the pituitary is barely open, thus restricting all but one-third of the brain from use.

So, by consciously reaching for more unlimited thought, which instantly stimulates the pituitary, we're creating new openings in the brain! Hang on now, because here's the brass ring: the moment we have more brain in use, no matter how tiny the newly used area is, we have just raised the frequency of our electromagnetic energy field and whammo! we can now pull in the higher frequencies of thought.

We're on our way to genius. The chain of events that will cause the brain to fully open has begun. The more brain that's open, the higher the frequency of incoming thoughts we can grab. The higher the frequency of thoughts, the more brain opens. This is the spiral that begins the awakening of our divinity.

As that little pituitary of yours begins to flower, things change in your life in ways you can hardly imagine. Your emotions come alive. You manifest more quickly. Your understanding grows. People may leave your life; others are drawn to you. You're in control. You're living in the moment, happy, in joy, and fulfilled.

So how do you begin? All you do is start reaching for those more unlimited, higher-frequency thoughts. Once they begin coming in, get ready for a high that will beat any pre-Program high to hell-and-gone, for as those faster vibrations activate new portions of your brain, you feel the flush of the hormone flow from head to toe. Like, wow!

Maybe you've just pulled in a terrific new thought, the kind you've never entertained before. It feels great! Or you've just realized something about yourself that's been hidden your whole life, and you're downright jazzed. You shout "Ya-hoo," or perhaps just drink in the expanded feeling with a "Well, I'll be damned! All right!"

At other times, as you start to pull in "higher" thought, you might feel washed (even socked) with intoxicating feelings that are like falling in love. They may last for a few minutes or even a few days. No matter, just acknowledge them, and enjoy. They're from the new hormone flow telling you the wake-up process has begun!

Why is all this so important? Well, your pituitary is the door to God. The more you allow unlimited thoughts into your brain, the more it opens. The more it opens, the more you know. And here's the crux of it: *whatever you know, you will become.*

Your world of problems will all but vanish because you're thinking differently. You'll be fed up with playing the victim role. You'll be in an altogether new playground and will frankly delight in creating its furnishings. And, by the way, once that pituitary is open, no matter the degree, it's open for all time!

The more you reach for expanded thought, the more will come, so stretch your mind to pull in those unlimited thoughts, about God, about you, about life, about love, about anything you're not used to thinking about. As you do this, there comes a sense of well-being for which there are simply no words. And physically, your body will have so much energy that at times you'll feel like you've been plugged into a vitamin socket.

This increase in physical energy is no coincidence. The surge in your energy flow comes as the new, higher-frequency thoughts come into the brain. As they enter, they shoot high-powered electrical currents through the central nervous system to every cell in the body, giving you that "wow" sensation as cells are recharged and revitalized.

Headaches, or what I call little "quick spikes," may be a temporary annoyance as the pineal in back of the head begins to swell from all this new energy coursing through your body. Or you may feel a little dizzy at times. But those are minor trade-offs for reaching into greater consciousness, for opening yourself up to the world of God that you are and from whence you came.

Of course, if you go on living according to everybody else's limited thought waves, the only part of your brain that will continue to be operational is that one-third which knows only struggle, survival, and judgment. More unlimited thought is out there waiting to come in, but you have to go after it if you want to change your life. So go after it, one step at a time, one frequency at a time.

The next obvious question is, can we open our brains completely? Absolutely! And it can happen in a moment, or it can take the rest of our lives. It doesn't matter. Every step we take to expand our minds brings us closer to that eventuality. Once fully opened, we have become the Mind of God, the Christ/Buddha/Mohammed consciousness which is within every one of us, waiting, pushing, urging us to become what we already are and have always been.

YOUR ELECTRIC LIGHT SHOW

Being, that which we are, is electronic. The God-reality, or God-presence, within and about us is a dazzling galaxy of light, a force field of supreme power.

Within the scientific community, the energy field surrounding the body is widely acknowledged to be a sort of two-sectioned system.

The first, which is closest to the body, is an electromagnetically charged field of high-frequency light that propels the electrical charges of thought *out* from within, and conversely, pulls *in* charges of thought from without, disbursing them in accordance with the brain's current operating frequency.

In the second, or outer, section, there are no divisions within the electrical units to sift out degrees of frequencies. In other words, in the outer field anything and everything comes in, unobstructed. It's an undivided light sphere of pure energy which allows all thought from the unending river of knowingness to flow through it.

Through this great outer field, which is connected directly to the Mind of God, we are forever in the conscious flow of all things that are known. Of course, precious little of that higher frequency flow can get through the inner fields since the brain's present receiving frequency is so low. And remember, the receiving frequency is directly related to the kind of thought we're allowing in, either social, conscious junk or higher-frequency expanded thoughts.

While the energy field is forever with us (it's what keeps us glued together, so to speak), it changes shapes and sizes and colors in accordance with our thoughts and with our emotions. In fact, this electric light show we put on is controlled primarily by our emotions, the energy force behind all thought. The more intense the emotion, the better the show, for the intensity of vibration of the electromagnetic waves has been increased. Get emotional, and suddenly you're putting on a better show than Futurama at Disneyland!

How often have you walked into a room full of people and wanted to turn right around and walk out? "Bad vibes," right? Or turn it around. When have you felt terrific in a room full of people? You've got it, "good vibes." Your energy field is picking up the vibrations coming from everyone else's energy fields. If you walk into a room of negative nerds and don't happen to be "down" there with them on that day, your field is most definitely going to feel it and send a minor shock wave throughout your body in the form of an emotional jolt, saying, "Hey, we don't fit here." The same thing in reverse is happening when you just love being with someone or some group. Your energy field is in tune with those about you, operating at the same vibrational frequency.

In Russia today, doctors are using the human energy field as a diagnostic tool. Knowing that illness is directly related to one's emotional state—therefore what one is thinking—they've devised a motion-picture camera to show, in the aura or energy field, the level of changing thoughts and emotions coming in and out of the patient's body. As the emotional intensity changes, the color, size, and pulsation of the energy field change, allowing the skilled diagnostician to quickly get to the hidden, trouble-causing beliefs that have probably raised havoc with the patient's body for years.

It's all energy! Everything we are, do, and think is energy. Attitude is energy. Desire is energy. Belief is energy. And it's transmitted solely by the intensity of emotion in back of it, magnetically charging up our "light show" in direct relation to the degree of emotion we're cutting loose.

With impassioned desire for more expanded thought, for instance, our vibratory frequency heightens, shooting highly charged thoughts out through our electromagnetic field and pulling back in those grand, unlimited thoughts of higher frequency.

Now the process begins. The pituitary kicks in, a tiny new segment of the sleeping brain opens ever so slightly, and instantly our electromagnetic energy field becomes more highly charged to draw new levels of experience into our world. Start to get the picture? Charge it up, shoot it out, pull it back, you open up.

Consciousness: The Unending Flow

You're standing high atop a lush green mountain field. All about you is wonderment, beauty, space, clouds, sky, and openness. The director in you yells "Action," you stretch out your arms to acknowledge the elements, toss back your head, and with a smile as big as the way you feel, whirl your body into hypnotic spins of care-free gaiety as gentle winds play through your hair and the sun presses its love and warmth into your being. The music begins to swell, you open your mouth, and out comes some joyous little ditty about the hills being alive.

It's all so heady, you feel if you inhaled hard enough you might actually be able to capture forever within your being the entire, glorious scene. Here, you know God lives within all things, for you can feel the reality of that power all around you. And you're right. What you're feeling is the highly charged essence of the All In All, which is more easily felt in a nature setting. What you're actually experiencing and breathing in is consciousness!

Consciousness is all about us. Our entire being, every cell in the body, is continually being fed by it. And thoughts come from consciousness. Consciousness is "aware-ized" energy, permeating the universe and every thing we see or know. By the same token, all energy is consciousness. So, what and where is your consciousness? Well, the fact of the matter is you're actually orbiting around yourself, your world, and your universe in countless numbers of very alive little units of energy.

Think of consciousness as the *parent* and thought as the *kids*. We create every moment of our existence with thought that comes from consciousness flow. Eventually the kids grow up to become the parents when they go back into the sea of consciousness flow.

In a like manner, consciousness consists of all thought that emanates from all beings and all things. And the thoughts that make up consciousness are of as many different electromagnetic frequencies as there are blades of grass in your yard, for there is no end to their span.

Consciousness, then, is the sum of all the different frequency values of thought, coagulating into matter only when enormously slowed down. And now here's the headline:

> *Each thought value attracts a like*
> *value to match its own frequency*
> *and intensity of feeling.*

This is the stuff of which our lives are made!!

Everything and everyone has thought patterns surrounding it. A social group or gathering of some sort will have its own type of pattern, as will a football crowd, or small town, or group in a bar. Cities as a whole, for instance, tend to have a heavier "social consciousness" pattern swirling around them, as there are more people in one place all thinking the same things: competition, time schedules, fashion consciousness, urgency, judgments, fearfulness. The wavelengths wherever you may be are all the same, so, without consciously controlling them, that's all you unconsciously pick up.

What do you think's so magic about "getting away from it all"? Why do more people vacation in nature settings, thronging to lakes, mountains, and beaches rather than cities? Because no matter how big the crowds may be at these nature resorts, the predominant thought patterns will be relaxation, peace, unwinding, contentment; so that's what you pick up.

The same is true at a baseball game, or an afternoon of golf. But try an extended vacation in Manhattan and see how long it takes before you're judging every clerk behind the counter, worrying about your spending, your travelers' checks, your attire, what time it is, how the kids are, or if your house sitter fed the cat. You're simply pulling in the frequencies around you while you blithely chalk it up to normal vacation-type thinking.

UP-OUT-UP-OUT-PUSH-2-3-4

Most of us were taught that consciousness is confined to the brain, or maybe even to our body cells. Who ever had any notion we should be trying to work with it and expand it? Expand it to where? Stretch it with what? And what for?

Our consciousness is like a muscle. To keep it healthy we need to exercise it, expand it, stretch it, use it, and these are not things most of us do with any degree of consistency prior to "waking up." Nor does stretching one's consciousness have anything to do with working Sunday's crossword puzzle. No, our consciousness comes alive by reaching out. Its natural bent is to do just that. It yearns to create, to reach and blossom into the higher frequencies of thought from whence it came. All we have to do is cut it loose and let it go.

As you begin to play with consciousness, exercise it, push it out to reach for those outrageous new thoughts, a marvelous phenomenon occurs; with increasing regularity you feel more up than down. Now that's a good enough reason to start "exercising," right there, but the main reason for stretching out is to become the powerful magnet we were intended to be.

The power to reach outward and become a part of the consciousness of the Whole is the gift of God to us all. To become that magnetic power center, we simply expand our force fields—our energy fields—by the conscious act of reaching, reaching, reaching for those new understandings.

Take a moment, if you like, and try this stretching exercise. Think of your consciousness—however or whatever you envision it to be—as flowing outward in endless circles from the center of your awareness to the periphery of infinity, your God-self awareness. Then, bring it back to the point of identity within you.

Again, feel it reaching out, seeking more of its awakening power. Feel the waves of consciousness going out in ever-widening circles, propelled by desire and want. See them and feel them reaching out, taking in more and more of the totality of All That Is until for one unspeakable, indescribable split second the waves are gone and you are merged with—you have become—the consciousness of God!

It's an experience you'll never forget when it happens, no matter how split the second. Everything kicks in, the pituitary, the brain, the higher frequencies being received. *What you're asking for is being drawn to you!* And once you've tasted that indescribable feeling, you'll go after it again and again.

If you live in a city, give yourself a helping hand now and then to stretch your consciousness, and go find nature in some form. Sit next to a tree. (The bigger it is, the more empowering will be your feelings.) Remember, consciousness in nature is much more elevated than in a city and can be more easily experienced. Go there, and let your mind stretch up and out to its very limits. And ask.

When you sincerely ask, for instance, to be filled with a consciousness which allows you to love everything you see and every thought you think (that's really stretching), and you ask it with a passionate depth of feeling, you immediately raise the vibratory frequency surrounding you. Bang! What's going out of you will now draw that love around you like bees to honey. That, in the truest sense, is expanding your consciousness.

Consciousness is like a flowing river, ever-moving, everchanging. You stand in the midst of this gentle current, every cell of your body being fed by the continuous flow of thought.

As you grow in your understanding of this river of thought (with which you create every moment of your existence), you may one day come to the same realization that I did, a realization so overwhelming that it still awes me; I no longer believe there is one molecule of my consciousness that is separate from God's.

Wherever there is life, there is consciousness, God expressing its own self-awareness. Consciousness is God's awareness of itself. All we have to do is reach into it.

THE SOUL OF YOUR BEING

Up to now, we've bandied about the term *soul* rather loosely, yet it's one of the most important aspects of what happens to incoming thought. So what is this thing called soul?

For years scientists have been baffled by the discrepancy in bodily weight just prior to, and immediately following, death. They can't account for about thirteen ounces which the body loses, sometimes immediately following clinical death, other times up to several hours after death. That discrepancy in weight is the soul, an incomprehensible powerhouse of electromagnetic creativity lodged in a cavity just next to the heart.

The soul, first and foremost, is the working duplicate of the Is (God). We are connected directly into the knowing of God's mind through the soul. Now, as soul relates to thought, its most important function is that of being the emotional memory bank of our being. And it's one *giant* memory bank.

Everything you can describe has certain feelings associated with it, and the soul has recorded every feeling from every last one of our emotional experiences. Memory is emotion (soul memory experienced), not data or events, and every emotion you ever had in this or any other lifetime is recorded in your soul, from the nostalgic scent of a blushing rose, to the panic of impending doom, or the splendor of a burgundy sunset.

In fact, that's how a thought is realized and known, through emotion. Since the thought of anything cannot be known until it's first felt, if it weren't for the soul that stores life's history of emotions, thoughts would pour right through us. There'd be no way for them to be classified and stored for future recall.

It's the soul, then, which gives our emotions validity. When a thought comes into us, it shoots through the brain, down through the central nervous system, then makes a beeline to the soul for memory recall. As soon as the soul receives the electronic units to be tabbed, it instantly searches through its memory banks for a "matchup," so the reasoning portions of the brain (what we would term intellect) can call it something with a word-match.

That single little thought that slipped in through your energy field was realized (felt) first in the totality of your body by cellular reaction, then flagged by the soul for shipment to the brain, which then formulated a word to describe the feeling.

But what happens when you pull in a totally new thought? The process is the same, except the new thought will carry a new emotion, one you haven't felt before. The new thought comes in to the brain (because now you're stretching your consciousness to receive higher thought), gets sent down throughout the body as a new buzz, then instantly to the soul for I.D. Whoops! "Cannot compute," says the soul. "We'll have to find a new label for this."

The new emotion, or feeling, is not currently stored in the soul because nothing like it has ever come in before. ("I have no words for what I felt.") Meanwhile, you're having some lightheadedness and feeling generally jazzed by a sensation you can't really describe.

The soul now has to take that new emotion and register it as being made up of higher-frequency thought. It will identify it in accordance with the brain's vocabulary, send it up to the brain, and presto! waking up is taking place. The grand new emotion is solidified within your being for instant recall the next time it's felt. No more lightheadedness the next time that thought comes in, because the new emotion is now a part of you.

If you'll stay alert to what you're feeling, you'll become more and more aware of those little awakenings taking place which are causing the whole of you to open up. Also be aware of the new things happening in your life, no matter how small. By consciously paying attention to these changes within and without, changes which you have brought about by your stretching to higher thought, you're pushing that pituitary to open more and the whole sequence of growth to expand.

Learn to listen and to trust. Your soul, in its infinite wisdom, knows what you need in order to evolve back into your oneness with God. That's the hunger you feel, from the soul's incessant pressing, pushing. That's its mission, to eradicate the seeming separateness from God (and it's had a pretty tough time of it for most of this lifetime). The key is to have faith that, regardless of what your soul may choose along the way for you to experience, it will ultimately take you Home, back to the God you are . . . remembered.

And don't worry about how to get there; your soul knows what to do; all you have to do is listen. If you're bored, it's telling you you've already done whatever you're doing now, and it's time to move on. If you long for a certain experience, it's telling you there's something in that experience for you to learn. So do it! It will be pushing at you relentlessly until you do. And if one of those strong yearnings within you right now happens to be your specific desire to reconnect with your Source, you have only to acknowledge that, then let your soul take you there. Most assuredly, it will!

Indeed, the wisdom of your soul, if left alone and allowed to function unencumbered, will bring about all the results in life and living you long for so earnestly. Just go within and listen to its direction. In the truest sense of the words, "let go and let God."

OUTGOING THOUGHT: MASTER DESIGNER OF OUR WORLD

One could easily write volumes on the studies of outgoing thought. In fact, with all the documented research available on the powers of thought, it puzzles me that we continue to live with so little control over our lives. Once we find out what happens to a thought when it leaves us, we have no more excuses. We'd have to have been lobotomized to make no attempt at changing our thinking. Be that as it may, "it takes what it takes," right?

Now, outgoing thought. When a thought we've received is ready to go back out, it does so most of the time through the brain, which sends it first to our energy field where it registers as an expectancy. Then the thought goes back out into consciousness flow to be picked up by someone else or to continue out into the omniverse. That expectancy, however, now activates the electromagnetic portion of our energy field to draw to us, with the force of a giant magnet, the likeness in frequency of whatever that attitude/thought may have been.

How's that again? Well, in simplest terms, what you send out is what you get back. Your field will magnetically attract—in some form—the same frequency of feelings experienced in your body at the time the thought left you. This could be a situation, object, event, or person. It makes no difference.

And the more intensely that thought or desire was felt before it left you, the more complete will be its fulfillment in your life. If you continue to have lousy relationships, or your checks forever bounce, or you never get a raise, or you're just generally blah, start paying attention to your thoughts! They are what's causing it all!

It's the old law of cause and effect. We draw to us what we think. If we're afraid of attack, we'll undoubtedly be attacked. If we're afraid of lack, we'll experience lack. Day after day, we create our world through our electromagnetically charged thoughts.

Yes, thoughts are magnets! They're not like magnets; they are magnets. And so are our beliefs, for a belief is a thought. They are electromagnetically charged when they leave us and dutifully go about their job of finding, or creating, a similarly charged event, person, or circumstance to match the belief we're sending out. Until we wake up and get rid of our long outdated, outmoded, overused beliefs and fears, what we get is exactly what we're sending out. In spades!

Visualize, for a moment, a little thought spitting out into your energy field. There it sits, charging your field and magnetizing itself into an expectancy. Beams from the magnetized area then radiate out in all directions like spray from a sprinkler hose, charged with their electromagnetic duty to "seek and return" their own match.

"My boss is mean," for instance, is an electromagnetically charged expectancy. "I can never find a good lover" is an electro-magnetically charged expectancy. "I hate being alone" is an elec-tromagnetically charged expectancy. "The kids never call" is an electromagnetically charged expectancy. "The math test will be a snap" is an electromagnetically charged expectancy.

Now, when you have *unlimited* thoughts, those that aren't tainted with doubt, fear, self-incrimination, etc., they go out from your *entire body*, not just through your brain. That's why loving thoughts (not sexual or addictive love, but just love-of-life type) make you feel so good. Your whole body gets into the act. But when the thought is one that has come from your reasoning, limited self, the only way it can get out is through the brain, which then trans-mits it in a much more limited manner.

That's not to say that brain transmission of limited thinking has no power. Hardly! It's only to say that unlimited thoughts of whole-being transmission have much more wallop. They're more highly charged, more highly magnetized. Your body is operating under God-self control, the supreme power of the universe.

EMOTION: THE GREAT PROPELLANT

You fly off the handle at someone or something, letting loose a stream of unprintable expletives. You sit by a crackling fire in abundant peace. You giggle lovingly at a baby's antics, thrill to a wild wind, speak unkindly of your neighbor, sit in catatonic silence in deep depression. It's all emotion, transmitting out from you in varying degrees of intensity. Emotion, the golden, secret key to thought's power.

While a thought is as alive as you and me, it's like a rocket without fuel until it has emotion behind it. It has no reality until it's felt in pure emotion. By the same token, it's thought that triggers the emotion and indicates how strong that emotion will be. We never speak a thought, for instance, until we've felt it. And that feeling is the *sensation* of the thought being realized through emotion. And around and around it goes.

So, while the thought of anything coming in can't be known until it's first felt (and identified), the same thing happens in reverse when we send a thought out. First we feel the emotion of it, not the actual thought itself. Then, once we have the emotion going, the brain translates it into an understanding for us by identifying it in our language of words, and out it goes, either through our whole being or through the brain.

Marvelous experiments have been made in projecting thoughts through massive steel barriers onto sensitized photographic plates without using cameras. (Thought easily passes through matter because of its frequency being higher than the mass through which it's passing.) These experiments clearly show the roll of emotion in transmitting thought. Unemotional thought records only blurred images on the film; emotional thought shows up as if painted by a detail artist. This is excellent proof that the stronger the emotion, the stronger the electromagnetic charge. And of course, the stronger the charge, the surer the return of the "match" of what you've sent, good or bad.

Emotion is always the propellant. And don't be misled into thinking that some casual thought such as "I wish my lover wasn't like that" doesn't have its emotional consequences. You don't have to be screaming emotion to be transmitting. What you're thinking, believing, or saying about yourself or another has *some kind* of emotion to it, whether you're aware of that emotion or not. Those beliefs, or unspoken (or spoken) thoughts are constantly transmitting emotions into your energy field as expectancies, beaming out to duplicate themselves in some form, come hell or high water.

WORDS TO LIVE BY

Every one of our dislikes, annoyances, judgments, delights, fears, and beliefs (known and unknown) is as real as a ten-ton truck, only a lot more powerful. The same is true of our spoken words, all those "thoughtless" little things we send out to create our reality day after day. Just as we are what we think, we are also what we speak.

Thoughts, spoken or silent, never die. At this very moment, all your tomorrows of bleak sameness or glorious newness are being formed by what your silent or spoken thoughts have been this day. You, and you alone, are writing your script. Want to change your life? Change your thoughts . . . including what you speak!

SUDDENLY YOU KNOW

And so our life is what we've caused it to be. Who's created all of our unhappiness? We have, by believing in it. Who's created our dis-ease, worry, misery and self-pity? We have, by believing in it. Who's created a life of lack? We have, by believing in it. We've lived in fear of everything and cried out to God for only a momentary taste of joy. If that's all we've asked for, that's all we've gotten.

You're on your way to Mastership, one step at a time, one day at a time. But that subconscious mind of yours will always take you where *it* wants to go, until you master your thinking *and* your speaking.

Know you stand at the point of choice. Take control of your awareness! If you don't, your subconscious will. And do you really want its worn-out beliefs running your life for evermore? I truly doubt it!

When you make the decision to take responsibility for what's happening—inside and out—there comes a moment when you know deep down inside that you alone created it, and you alone can change it. Oh, what a sweet moment that is! Now you begin to create in a way that makes you happy, in fact downright joyous. What else do you think God—which is the life you are—wants for you but happiness, pure, exuberant, endless, empowered, creative, dynamic happiness? All you have to do is want it, then know it to be so, and the rest will follow as surely as night the day.

If you want to be closer to the reality of what you are, you have only to raise the nature of your thoughts. The higher the thoughts you go for, the more unlimited the thoughts you get; the more unlimited the thoughts you maintain, the more life you'll experience without struggle. There comes immense clarity and ease of purpose in your life. It's just damn fun being alive!

CHAPTER 6
YOUR INNER BEING

Letting go of fears, letting go of guilts and limitations, letting go of unending patterns of unproductive habit, my God, what would that be like? Hard to imagine, isn't it? Yet without that letting go, life remains filled with old ideas, mercilessly holding us victim to the past, or to people, places, and things.

Enough of that old stuff! It's time to remember, and put to use, our long-forgotten powers of divinity.

Why don't we remember our Godhood? Why do we still live in the dark ages of superstitious beliefs and binding dogma? Why do we so ardently refuse to believe in our own omniscience?

Well, how could it be otherwise? We believe what we've been told, and for eons we've been told we were the lowest of creatures while God, the Almighty, was the supreme power out there. When was the last time you were taught, in church or anywhere else, that God was *not* an essence apart from you, but the Isness of ongoing life and thought, the very life-force of your divine and eternal self? Not lately, I'll bet.

Long, long ago we forgot the greatness of that essence within us. Power groups (better known as churches) hungrily played on that forgetfulness to their own glorification. We learned of fear and death, but forgot life. We learned of sorrow and pain, but forgot joy. We learned of humanness, but forgot God, the ongoingness and foreverness within us which our minds can't understand but our hearts already know.

This is a road into that remembering. It's our bridge to the highest thought and emotion that created these bodies of ours so that God, our Higher Power within and without, might experience Itself in this form called human. It's a journey into Self, for as we awaken into our true reality and blossom into our Godhood, we are also blossoming into our Selfhood, our real, unlimited Selves.

I wanted so much to love God and be loved by God. Never for a moment did it enter my head that I was seeking what I already was! And it certainly never occurred to me that the imageless being which is my very essence was the same omnipresent power of the universe, indeed, of the omniverse, the collectiveness of all that is.

There is no parallel in our experience of life to help us understand this power. How does one fathom creation? Yet it's within us, an ever-present reservoir of creative vitality, understanding, serenity, love, and universal energy, ready to spring into reality the moment we put out the call. It's what we are. It's our God within, our Inner Being.

If you haven't had to wrestle at some time on the Program with who and what your Higher Power was, my hat's off to you. While most of us do finally come to some sort of comfortable concept of our Higher Power, it's usually been with some degree of struggle. Old programming from church and family, along with early beliefs from childhood of flowing robes and long white beards, all merged to form the concept we brought to the Program and had to contend with, often for a painful length of time.

"We came, we came to, we came to believe," is how it happened for the vast majority of us with the help of our sponsor, some urgent soul-searching, a rabbi, priest, or minister, and a batch of after-meeting coffee klatches. Oh sure, we've all known those happy beings who came sailing into meetings like Peter Pan without a care in the world except their addiction, insisting that God had always been a friendly, known quantity to them, and telling us how their relationship with their Higher Power was now nothing short of exquisite. Well, that wasn't my story, and my guess is it wasn't that way for the majority of us.

While most of us held some sort of belief in a God, many of us were agnostic; witness that chapter in the Big Book. And we've all known those who have remained agnostic, sober, and moderately content after many, many years of working the Twelve Steps. More power to 'em.

Indeed, most of us come to the Program in as many stages of God-awareness as we do in degrees of addiction, but the one element that quickly binds us together, in addition to our common problem, is our need to find a belief in our "God as we understand Him." We soon learn that if we want to stay clean or recovering from whatever, we'd better get it together with this Higher Power business. In one form or another, most of us have done that. But we've run aground. By so often placing that precious life-giving Power *out there*, we've run aground.

Be honest now. Wouldn't you agree that, with few exceptions, our Higher Power has been no more a part of us than the cars we drive (and called on much less frequently)? Though it's almost always come to our rescue when called upon, we've gone to our

Higher Power only in times of need. It's been *out there* to be sought, thanked, blamed, or chatted with, but only when appropriate, only when necessary. We keep seeing our Higher Power as *greater than*, therefore separate from us, apart from us. That it is greater than our ego-selves is surely a truth, *but we can no longer continue to see ourselves as being only that ego identity.* We are vastly, vastly more.

As long as we perceive ourselves as separate from the God of our beings, our egos are in control of our thoughts, drawing into our lives event after bleak event of repetitious unpleasantness. Again and again, in agony or anger, we seek the help of our Higher Power, only to cut it loose once the help has come, then fall right back into hot soup again. Same game, new players, same old pain. Can you honestly say you want to keep that up? I can't imagine why!

So here's the heart of it. Separation from the God of our being, from what we are, is the single greatest cause of emotional pain on the face of the Earth.

If we had only known we had this wonderful inner teacher we could turn to, and turn it over to, an inner teacher which is as much a part of our Higher Power as our finger is of its hand, we might have changed our thinking and forever stopped looking out there for answers from God as we understood Him, not to mention looking outside to people, places, and things.

The majority of us have been earnest believers, but only part-time users. While "we came to believe" has been the path to life for hundreds of thousands of us, we find one day that behind our beliefs lay a hollowness, an indefinable void. Even after years on the Program, pain continues to plague us. And we keep calling it growth? Nonsense! How can growth come from the same old pain?

No, that hollowness we're feeling is the separation from, and denial of, our essence. And so comes that deep urging from within saying, "Enough! I want to go from my darkness and from my fear. I want to go to my oneness, and my joy, and my peace. I no longer want that hollowness. I no longer want to feel separate!"

BEHOLD GOD

So who are we? Well, the reality of who and what we are is far beyond these selves we think we know. One thing's for sure; we are not our bodies.

We see ourselves as a body that works, plays, dresses, loves, and thinks. In reality, each of us is a portion of the infinite, a glorious piece of God destined to wake up one day and become the real us. We are an immense collective mass of energy in a form of identity. We are the unlimited, unexplainable Source experiencing life here on Earth in human form. We are the power and consciousness of All That Is, God. *That* is our true identity.

So, as *part* of the Whole, what God is, we are. Can you say that, because your parents are human, you are then butterfly? Of course not. You are of the human species, therefore human. You are of God, therefore God. You are a fiery, pure, energy force of light, living inside that vehicle, your body, to obtain the prize of creative life, the emotional (gut-level) understanding that life is communication with God, and communication with God is life. Indeed, you are Life, a portion of God struggling to rid itself of ego and return to the totality of its being.

Step Two says we "came to believe that a Power greater than ourselves could restore us to sanity" (Alcoholics Anonymous 1975, 59). A power greater than our ego-selves, yes, but a power greater than our real selves, no! We are *not* less than. *We are not less than!*

In fact, to accept ourselves as less than is downright arrogant, for it means we believe our inflated ego-evaluation of ourselves is truer than God's! Can't be so.

So we run around searching desperately for value, when in truth, our value needs no defense. It merely is. We exist as the mind of God which cannot be separate from us; it is us. There is not now, nor has there ever been, a separation between any one of us and God, except as devised and reinforced by the ego.

All of life is God! And we are life, here, there, everywhere. God is outside us as the light source from which to draw, and God is connected to us through the oneness of consciousness and thought. Yes, there is a power greater than ourselves, only *we are a part of that power,* ever changing, ever creating, ever expanding, ever being. God is the Whole of Life, evolving, ongoing into forever. God is man and woman. God is our Inner Being. God is you. Behold God!

THE GOD OF OUR YOUTH

Think back for a moment on what your concept of God was when you were a youngster, and keep that concept apart from the understanding you hold today of your Higher Power. Did you see God as a judging entity, critical of good and evil, frowning and thundering at sin? To have been raised in a church of strong beliefs is not easy to overcome; sin, evil, devil, Hell, damnation, and fear, fear, fear. Or did you see your God as a loving, understanding, and forgiving force, full of fun, friendship, and beauty?

However we viewed our God, so did we view ourselves.

If we saw God as judgmental, we not only lived in fear of that judgment but spent a major portion of our lives in unending judgment of others, and worse, of ourselves. If our God was one who saw only good and evil, then good and evil (right and wrong) is how we equated the actions of others and ourselves. The separation became acute. Now look what happened. The more we feared our God, the greater grew our self-image as being imperfect, wrong, the greater became our day-to-day anxiety, and the greater grew our separation.

"I'm not good enough" became the subconscious platform on which most of the activities in our lives were based. Talk about low frequency! We've walked through life as one big, social-consciousness receiver-transmitter. Since that's all we projected, that's all we pulled in, repetitious circumstances that were consistent reflectors of our beliefs.

Had we only known we were not separate from what we already are, our lives would have been quite different. We would not have seen life as being good or bad. No, we would have seen all life as God, as just *being*.

We would not have seen ourselves as right or wrong, but simply as unfolding Gods, living out lessons to be learned, forever creating new adventures.

So, what *is* your concept of God? If your God is a heavenly dictator, you're going to see yourself as disconnected and powerless. If your God is judgmental, you're into merciless self-judgment. If you see your Higher Power as a partner, that's closer to the truth but still perpetuates separation.

It's time to know that you are one with the infinite. Chew on the concept. Play with it. Know with everything in you that you are not apart from, separate from, or alone. Never have been; never will be.

WHAT ARE WE DOING HERE?

Not too many years ago there were three kinds of people who caused my heart to ache. The first were the constant "slippers," the poor souls who could just never seem to get their you-know-what together to stay sober. The second were the ones who had just gotten whitewashed in a relationship, losing their other half to a carnivorous new love.

While all of me longed to find some way to relieve the pain my friends in those first two groups were experiencing, nothing, but *nothing*, could compare to the compassion I felt for the poor, misguided souls who talked about life after death and previous lives. In my deepest imaginings I could not conceive of people being so misinformed, or living in such a Never-Never Land of wishful thinking. Were their lives so empty as to need this fanciful projection of a continuum of life? It baffled me.

Since the days at my High Sierra lake when I leaped into this new way of thinking and passioned to unfold into the God I am, there has not been one stretch of time when I haven't been actively involved in its study in one form or another, study which has led me to a humble change of opinion of my third group of friends.

These truths are now mine. I ask only that you attempt to be somewhat more open to them than I was, for the concepts surely explain what we're doing here in the first place.

We come into a bodily life raring to go, ready to remember, eager to correct this outdated sense of separation from our reality. We come to create a full, happy life, not one of struggle and drudgery engendered by fear. We come to train our minds to be in tune with their own vast energies. Then we get socked with social consciousness, and we slow to a near stop in our learning and inner desire for remembrance.

But life goes on, consciousness goes on, and we go on. We're in this thing called evolution for however long it takes us to wake up to that point of oneness. And even then, life goes on, and we go on, and on, and on.

Though we've all been around this track before (quite a number of times, it appears), we've not been too swift at getting the message. Happily, the overdue process of waking up is beginning all around us. Fear of death is rapidly giving way to the realization that this is not the only shot we're going to have at this business of being in a body. We've done it before and will likely do it again until all the lights are on. In the meantime, we've been given the power to create whatever we might desire, from the vilest of things to the loveliest of things, in our search for understanding and joy. That's our God-given free will in full swing.

There are no directives from on high. It's all freewill choice. Nor did we return to balance out some ghastly thing we may have done in 9007 B.C. We returned because we wanted to move ourselves toward our oneness with God.

The time is here on this planet for us to do just that. The wake-up call has gone out to stop living hit-or-miss, to take back our power, and remember who and what we are! The call has gone out to *come Home!*

So here we are, flesh and blood, clothed and endowed with the Light of God to experience through the human drama. And joy of joys, as we come to believe in the concept of ongoing consciousness, we begin to relinquish that blind fear of dying that carries with it such an inordinate fear of living. How can we be afraid of life if we know it goes on into eternity?

Granted, the ideas might take some getting used to, but that's fine. Take them with ease, a little at a time. If they fit, wonderful;

then your life just found its purpose. If not, well that's a choice. There's always another go-around.

FILLING THE VOID

Somewhere along the line of growing up, we acquired the idea that being lonely is positively not OK. It's sort of like the youngster who mopes around the house for some reason and Mom says, "What's wrong, Honey?" "I dunno, I just feel all alone." Maybe he's afraid of something and doesn't know how to express his feelings to Mom. So Mom says, "Well, go do something. Go watch TV or have a piece of cake. You'll feel better."

Feeling lonely never has been, and is definitely not now, OK in most social circles, so, like the child, we never get a chance to really feel the feelings. Instead, we end up stuffing them. Then, just as the youngster had no one to go to for comfort, we're left alone with the lostness and nowhere to put it.

Didn't you ever wonder why the topic of isolation was such a hot favorite at meetings? Or why we even need such a topic in the first place? Why, when we have a Higher Power to turn to, would we ever decide to hide in a TV set or behind a stack of paperbacks for evenings on end, and isolate ourselves? Sure, we've all done it. But why? Why would we choose to turn our backs on our Higher Power, friends, and family, when such actions only serve to heighten the very emptiness we're trying to fill?

Well, for one thing, we get mighty tired carrying the load of victimhood, and don't know how to unload it. We feel *apart from* because we've forgotten we're a part of the divine, that there's no difference between humanity and divinity. We isolate ourselves because we're not too wild about our own company, this outer self-image we keep working at so diligently. We're in a void and don't know how to fill it.

Let's see if we can put this God-self thing in perspective in relation to emptiness. Take a moment and envision a mammoth sphere, maybe five hundred miles in diameter. In the center is a dot no bigger than a pinprick. See the sphere expanding out into the universe, its borders starting to evaporate in the expansion. Soon they don't even exist, and the mass of the sphere is free to roam into forever, joining the frequencies of infinity. And what of that little pinprick in the middle? It's still there, the same size, totally oblivious to the power and grandeur of the mass that surrounds it, flows through it, is it.

The expanding mass is the real you, the God of your being. And the little dot is the ego-self, kept small by its lack of remembering. The minute we remember we're the whole sphere, no more loneliness, no more need to be isolated. That emptiness or void within no longer exists!

Remembering is like a knowingness that wells up inside you. Call for that knowingness, find it, and pay attention to it, and it will tell you clearly what you want to know. Call for that knowingness, and it will allow you to feel loved beyond imagination, eradicating pain, loneliness, and unworthiness. Set your doubts aside as to whatever that knowingness within may be; it's as real as you are, because it's what you are.

So how do you get started? By asking! It's that simple. The more you ask, and the more you turn your attention towards your desire to know, to feel, to remember that presence, the more your desire will become an expanding awareness that will never leave you and never stop expanding. But asking comes first. If you don't ask, nothing will happen.

When I first started this journey, I kept on only because I had experienced that miraculous change of attitude from gut-wrenching loneliness to astonishing peace in the space of one week. Obviously, something had worked, but I didn't know what to label it. The little book that was my companion at the lake said it was God within me, but the concept was too foreign for me to understand. God had always been *out there*, and to think that some sort of power within had manifested this miracle was this side of impossible to believe.

Nonetheless, something had happened, and the results seemed to be holding. If I was to keep the void filled on a permanent basis, I knew I had to make a permanent shift in my thinking. So I made the decision to go for it and relentlessly asked for help. The result of that decision—and asking—has been awesome beyond words.

SHIFTING GEARS: BEYOND STEP THREE

Shifting a car with a stick shift takes a little getting used to if you've never done it before. But there's no feeling like it in the world when you smoothly push that handle into high gear and feel the power come alive. All it takes is practice. If you have the willingness to shift your thinking from *out there* to *in here*, all you need is a little practice, and it's done!

Take, for instance, an issue in your life that's unpleasant, or even painful, and let that issue become your first practice right now with shifting. Remember, you have a new Partner, your Higher Power within, the God that you are. It's just a shift of focus, from *out there* to *in here*. Ask that power to darn-well manifest itself in your life . . . now! And keep asking.

Now when you "let go and let God," know you're letting go to your Inner Being, as well as to the power of the universe. They're the same. No more autopilot into oblivion. No more being out of control in your life. And no more giving up responsibility to powers apart from you, which perpetuates the empty feeling of separation.

What we're doing here is shifting gears and taking Step Three to a new level. We're not changing it, just expanding it. Step Three says, "Made a decision to turn our will and our lives over to the care of God *as we understood Him*" (Alcoholics Anonymous 1975, 59). Absolutely, only now we're reaching inside to create our lives with the help of our Higher Power (Inner Being) of which we are a part, rather than solely Higher Power *out there*, which means separateness.

The moment we let that force move around in us, daring to feel it, we've put an expectancy into our energy fields that says, "By golly, my Higher Power and I *are* one. It does exist in me, as well as about me." A new feeling of love and strength fills every crevasse of separateness, or aloneness. We've turned our will and our lives over to the care of God within, as well as God without, the same inseparable power.

After you finish this section, you might want to close your eyes for a moment and see if you can sense within yourself the great energies of your Inner Being. Let yourself experience the joy of those energies. Reach way down. You're sitting on powerful emotions of love, compassion, understanding, and warmth that want to come out, the emotions and frequencies of your Inner Being.

Tap in, then see those emotions going out from you in multidirectional waves, for indeed they do. (As you become more proficient in this emotional visualization, the intensity, and therefore the perceived distance, of the waves increases by quantum leaps.) See if you can actually sense the bands of electromagnetic energy radiating out from deep within you to search for their higher frequency match. You're creating; new events, new people, new feelings, new world!

In this shifting of focus, everything begins to change. Even those heavy issues you've been dealing with start to dissipate. It may take a few tries, but once you touch ever so lightly the core of emotion that wells up from experiencing your own vastness, it gets easier and easier to bring forward. The experience is indescribable! You're raising your own frequency to call forth your own powers. You're on your way.

So, close your eyes now, if you'd like. Reach down, feel, sense. Shift your focus within, going for that still, quiet place where nothing is impossible. Nothing! Go for the place where the strength and love of the God you are abide. If tears come, wonderful! Let them come; you're connecting! If you feel you're not getting there, just repeat to yourself, "My Inner Being knows the way and is leading me." Indeed, that's a great truth. You're turning your will and your life over to the care of your Higher Power within, as well as without . . . You!

THE IMPORTANCE OF ACKNOWLEDGMENT

We're sort of like a piece of electrical equipment that's just come off the assembly line, ready to operate but needing to get plugged in. As you plug into the power of You, new energies come into play, and things start to happen in your life.

Whenever these times come, by all means acknowledge them and say "thanks." Acknowledging the newnesses in your life, whether emotions or events, sends loud and clear messages to your subconscious that changes are actually taking place. The acknowledgments register in your soul, raising you up a notch on the frequency scale. Before you know it, you're pulling in even higher-frequency consciousness, along with its new everything else—events, people, emotions, circumstances, etc.

So be alert for ways to expand your awareness, your consciousness. Then, when happenings come into your world that once may have caused panic, you'll be amazed at how smoothly you handle them. You'll no longer feel helpless. In fact, your reactions will probably be quite foreign to you. Happy days! You're operating from inside out. Not only your attitude but every cell in your body is being changed by the waves of higher frequency coming in!

And whatever you do, please don't negate your accomplishments by chalking them up to coincidence! Pat yourself on the back. It was you who called those insights, or changes, or happenings forth, and they're most surely not coincidence.

All Heaven Supports Us

Does the God of our Being hear us? Always! Remember, the divine communication link within us can never be broken, and that link is as mighty today as it was eons ago when first we came as sparks of Light from Thought. We need only practice trusting its council and know the answers already exist. So, does the God of our Being hear us? It cannot be otherwise!

In fact, help comes from many sources in the Isness once we ask. It comes automatically from projecting our higher electromagnetic frequencies, and it comes from those frequencies being received by unseen consciousness in higher cosmic realms.

Consider the power we are stretching from within to beyond
infinity, which means when we go within, we automatically draw
from without. In other words, since our thoughts, in the form of
requests, project everywhere, they're constantly being received by the
cosmic energies which surround us.

But since the universal law of free will precludes assistance
until it's requested, we've got to ask! Then look out, for once the
request is made from the depths of one's heart, all heaven stands
ready to hold our hands in guidance, open doors, bring new people
into our paths, and press intuition into our awareness. In fact, the
cosmic help which surrounds us in these times of awakening consciousness is stacked umpteen deep, waiting only for us to ask.

Then, once you've got that request out there, tune in and listen. The simple act of asking your Inner Being for anything automatically raises your frequency, ensuring a response regardless of
how it gets to you. So listen to everything, your feelings, your intuition, happenings, or clues and messages from any source.
Granted, you may not have answers right away, but they'll come.
Just trust, watch, and listen. All heaven will stand in support of
your endeavors.

WHOSE WILL, MINE OR GOD'S?

I can't think of a bigger favorite, as far as Program topics go,
than "How do you know whose will—yours or God's—is the 'right'
will in any given situation?" Meeting topic, sponsor topic, after-
hours topic, in-your-shower topic. Of course, if the issue had ever
been resolved, it wouldn't keep coming up with such urgent
frequency.

First, let's clarify a few of the conflicting terms that seem to surface when this topic is discussed in a group meeting. For instance, willpower. What does willpower have to do with God's will?

Very simply, willpower is not a creative force; willpower is ego power from our outer self rather than from our Inner Being. Willpower is a function of the intellect, and as such, surely has a place in the order of creativity, but is exceedingly weak in its ability to make things happen.

Then there's free will. This is altogether different, for free will is all will. It's what we were given to create with in order to explore all dimensions of thought. We've been given free will to expand our consciousness into a greaterness, so to speak, for as we expand, so does the mind of God.

With free will, we can explore this thing called Mind, break out of our limited ego thinking, and return to the Light of our being. Free will is the purest form of love God gives us, to be, do, and create our world as we choose. And without exception, that's just what we've done, chosen every one of our circumstances by our own free will.

The key, then, to the question of whose will is to reign lies in acquiring the ability to listen. In listening to the voice of our heart, we're listening to our Inner Being, our real Self. Trust that force within, and you're trusting God's will. It's that simple. All we have to do is listen to it and trust its direction; then *our will and God's will are always the same.*

So how do you know when it's not your ego kicking up? By listening and feeling, by that inner sense. As you build the bridge of trust to your Inner Being, you'll easily see how your deepest desires, urges, and hunches are really the will of God expressing. It's that feeling of alignment, sort of like an inner "clunk" that says, "Yeah! That's it!"

Now your desires begin to happen because nothing in your energy field is in contradiction. It's like being cleared for takeoff. Your engine's revved, the controls are set, and everything's cleared for "Go." Your "want" is being attracted to you by a clean, aligned, energy surge. The expectancy in your energy field is of a high frequency, and results happen . . . like now! You're calling forth the rearrangement of your life, with all systems "Go!"

Remember, it's not "God's will" you are where you are. It's your will, which is God's. In other words, it's not "His fault out there." Nor can we cleverly sidestep a decision that may loom ahead of us by copping out and leaving it up to God's will, or the "Whatever is 'right' will be," litany. The responsibility for our lives comes to rest squarely on our shoulders, for our shoulders and God's are one and the same.

With a little practice, spotting the difference in *wills* will soon be easy. You'll feel comfortable about your decisions, for when your free will isn't tied up with that roustabout ego-self, there's less struggle. You're no longer bucking the flow of everyday life. By quietly choosing the direction that seems to be the most harmonious with your God within, you're in tune, and the feeling is sweet. Often you'll find it's the feeling that gives you the greatest joy. Some call it intuition, or knowingness. Whatever you call it, you're riding the current of consciousness of the Is. You're operating off of God's will.

I have a friend who speaks of her "sense" of things. "I have a sense that I am to let go of this right now." Or, "My sense is that I need to be there next week." I love that phraseology, for she's tuning into, and speaking directly from, her knowingness, her Inner Being. She's operating off of God's will.

The test here is trust, and it's no small item, for to "let go and let God" is the complete trusting of your intuitive rather than conscious mind to guide you. It's the *knowing* that when the time is right, you'll be presented with the wisdom you require. Knowing and trusting. Knowing and trusting. Not an easy task for those of us who have diligently followed the path of "self-will run riot."

So when some difficulty comes up, stop, take a big breath, and look at it. If you have options, but don't like any of them and feel confused, hold off making a decision. Give yourself some slack, taking ample time to go within where you can make a deep, inner decision. Sit with the whole situation as you see it. Then put a smile on your face and allow the answers to come. Intuitively you'll begin to sense the probable choices, knowing instinctively which are most harmonious with your own inner direction. Indeed, "the answers will come if your own house is in order" (Alcoholics Anonymous 1975, 164).

Intuitive thought, by the way, comes directly from the mind of God, so it's a higher frequency than everyday thought. Learn to trust that it's not made up, and you'll never again have a question as to whose will you're following. You'll always know. That old, frantic serenity drops away, and there comes a quietness, a sureness, one day at a time.

When finally you can say, "God's will is my will," you put logic aside. You stop thinking of God's will as a thing apart from yourself. You turn it over, simply enough, to that voice inside that knows. At that moment, you've taken your biggest leap into freedom and mastery.

Bit by bit, step by step, you're moving closer to your Source, walking into moments that are impossible to describe in their awesome newness. Desire these moments with everything in you and embrace them when they come. Listen to and trust your knowingness. Then remember for all time, you cannot separate from that which you already are, your Inner Being which is God, your Inner Being which is You.

CHAPTER 7

THE EGO: MASTER OF COVER-UP

You're seated in a classroom being taught by two professors of diametrically opposing views. There's no discourse, no arguing between them. One believes one way and teaches it; the other believes the opposite way and teaches it. One seems powerful and sure, yet the other has a louder voice. You emotionally lean toward the one you can hear the easiest, but you're never sure. You're just . . . never . . . sure.

Two teachers of opposite views teaching one class? Absurd! You'd get nowhere except into a state of constant confusion, right?

Right! And this is what's been happening to us since the day we were born. Taught to mistrust intuition that comes from our inner voice, we went with what seemed to be real to us, our character, or ego-selves, that image we so carefully worked at building since early child-hood. That was real. If we could touch it, smell it, feel it, hear it, see it, or taste it, that made it real. Any gut-level feelings, hunches, or insights that might have emerged to guide us were rarely considered valid.

All of our lives, those same two voices have been going off inside us, one from our God-self, the other from our ego-self. Most of the time we've responded only to the ego-self, the one which nurtures and maintains that cherished image. We've known no other way to live, or to survive.

Yet we've become totally lost in that image. The images of the macho man or the flighty woman, for example, are not personality traits. They're ego-created characters which we stand on our heads to maintain. The personality, on the other hand, is real, a part of the core of our Inner Being.

Our personalities are our pure Selves, but the image is from the ego. It alone is the cause of our separation from the God of our being. The image is made up of our fears and judgments. The image is all of our negative, limited thinking, for it has no other basis of truth. The image is our need to be needed and loved, for it has no idea how to tap the true love of its own reality.

Somewhere along the way of our lives, we buried ourselves in this image and forgot our divinity. We became our image, turning our backs on our real selves. The frantic scramble ever since has been to maintain that identity at all costs lest we become nothing.

Fortunately, we do hear that inner voice at times, or most of us would never have gotten to the Program. But rare indeed have been those callings from within that we listened to with rapt attention and then chose to follow. Now it's time to make a choice. We cannot keep listening to those two teachers of opposing views and expect to grow into an awareness of Self. It will never happen.

THAT CLEVER, IRASCIBLE EGO

Character, image, ego-self, outer-self, call it what you will. If this ego of ours is what has caused the separation from our real Selves, why do we have it anyhow?

The ego is the tool we've been given to test the strength of our desire to evolve back to the Light. But instead of working with us, the ego has fearfully perceived itself as separate, completely on its own. It learned at an early age precisely how to control our private world to ensure we remain in a constant state of struggle. We all know only too well that marvelous Program expression, "self-will run riot." Well, in a broader sense, our ego is free will run riot. It's the cunning, lovable troublemaker of our being that's just gotten way out of hand. We have this perpetual image of ourselves, this *being* we think we want to be with all the labels. That's the ego, forever drawing to it circumstances and events to reinforce the image. For all its power, though, our ego is really nothing more than an irascible brat over whom we've exercised little or no control up to now. It'll do everything it can to weigh us down with those very beliefs we want to give up, hollering bloody murder the moment we attempt to remove them.

Happily, the ego doesn't have to be obliterated to continue this journey, just soundly and lovingly put in its place. While we can almost always expect a fight at the entrance to every new level of spiritual development, as long as the ego sees itself evolving along with the rest of its being and not left behind, it will usually throw in the towel and go along.

THE ENDLESS LIST

Almost every moment of every day, that ego keeps us in separation, feeling we're *apart from*. The million and one limiting thoughts we have minute to minute are straight from the ego. For instance:

- The ego thinks it's perfectly normal to point out someone else's mistakes and to correct them. What better way for it to feel superior?

- The ego has a big-time investment in sickness. Even though a sick body is unnatural to the real Self, with sickness, the ego can continue to feel vulnerable.

- The ego wants us to think that our problems are real, solvable only with its own mighty logic, which is almost always based in fear.

- The ego is an expert in confusion, knowing perfectly well we can't live happily with two inner voices pounding at us day after day.

- The ego thrives on guilt, and it couldn't care less whether that guilt belongs to its owner or to somebody else.

- The ego adores sacrifice and reasons that sacrificing itself to the good of any relationship makes it powerful.

- The ego tries to tell us how foolish we are in attempting to grow spiritually, for it knows this way of life means learning to love from the inside out, an utter contradiction to the ego's modus operandi.

- The ego delights in reinforcing beliefs in our own insignificance.

- The ego goes to any lengths to maintain our identity as a struggling victim of circumstance. And you can bet it would never even remotely consider suggesting a way out.

- The ego specializes in keeping things complicated and delights in hiding what might be obvious solutions.

- The ego is a past master at intellectualizing, one of its more reliable separation ploys.

In fact, any reaction you have that's based in fear comes from the ego-self, not the God-self. And since everything on this plane which is not love is fear, there's one whale of a spectrum of emotions being encompassed.

On and on the ego goes, keeping us deep in its fear-based image, as far away from our loving core as possible. It's ruled our lives with high-handed, freewheeling abandon since the day we were born, pumping distorted beliefs into the subconscious, shouting for all its worth to override our God-given intuition, and clapping its hands with glee at our acquiescence to its demands. It's time to take control of this imp once and for all! But be warned; your ego's not going to give up easily. It's not going to like this new approach to life. Not one bit!

Pain: The Biggest Ego Illusion

Most of us have a human self-awareness which is an awareness of the self as the ego. Up to now we've known no other self, no other will, no other consciousness than that of the ego. Since the ego is not sustained by a force outside itself (i.e., God, Higher Power, etc.), it naturally holds self-preservation to be its only reason for being, when in actuality the ego is nothing more than a belief about ourselves. But remember, as we believe, so we are, and so we attract.

High on the list of favorite beliefs we cater to, for example, is pain, one of the ego's favorite illusions. Yes, illusion! For most of us, pain is what we think we need to grow. (I was absolutely convinced of it. "Pain is the touchstone of growth" was a favorite mantra of mine from the podium.) Indeed, we see pain as a normal part of life. But to allow our pain to become a comfortable, intellectual habit is nothing short of insanity. And that's all pain is, an intellectual habit, without exception the worst addiction in any form known to mankind!

Pain is simply negative thought built around an imagined future event that comes from the remembrance of a past experience. And there we are, constantly trapped between two points that don't exist, future and past!

We say this "feels good" or that "feels bad," but where did we get this information in the first place? We learned it from past experience. In fact, "good" and "bad" are only judgments derived from our past, and all judgments are learned.

Emotional pain, then, as we know it, is nothing more than a judgment, and like any judgment, is a learned response, not a fact. *Pain is not a fact!* It's an intellectual habit born of a learned response.

A memory comes up of our past, and we say, "Ooh, I don't want to look at that; it's too painful." But reason it out; the event may have been real, but the pain we've built around it is not an actual fact! It has no power! Yet in our fear of experiencing that imagined pain, we run around hiding ourselves from the world, diligently stuffing the pain deeper and deeper into our subconscious, rather than bringing it out and dealing with it. Hiding and stuffing, two sure ways to maintain our painful addiction to pain. What a circle!

Of course, our ego says this is the normal, safe way to go, constantly reacting to the past and fearing the future. It demands we look everywhere but the Now, for in the Now is the connection with divine power which is the high vibratory frequency of love, a frequency that's sure death to the ego, therefore sure death to pain.

Oh hey, who among us hasn't known excruciating, emotional pain? Pain of past events, pain of lack, pain of relationships, pain of looks, pain of low self-esteem—they've all been realities to us in one degree or another. And it would seem the greater our insistence on proving how real that pain is, the more we have identified with the illusion of it. So we get trapped, can't see the forest for the trees. Over and over we keep drawing the pain to us, convinced we're hapless victims of circumstances, with no way out.

The trick now is to decide if painful thinking makes us happy. Don't laugh! Nine times out of ten we confuse suffering with happiness! As long as we're living in the ego, and not through the Inner Being where the *us* that we want to be really lives, we unconsciously misinterpret suffering as our normal way of life. In other words, we confuse our pain with happiness!

Contrary to what you may think, emotional pain is not a necessity in one's life, no matter what your past may have been. It is not a requirement of growth, it is not the irreversible result of your childhood, nor is it normal! It can be corrected in the same manner we correct any other addiction. First we recognize it, then we go to work on it.

FEEL AND RELEASE

Right up there next to the word *pain* is *hurt*. "I'm hurting"—favorite words around a meeting or with a sponsor. How often we say or think those words without the slightest idea what the reality is behind them or what power we're giving to the thought. Suffice it to say for now that, like pain, hurt has no power. It has no mind of its own. *Hurt* is an exercise; that's all it is. We need only go inside, speak to our Inner Being, and insist it be removed. If we do that regularly, no matter how severe the pain, or how ancient, or how justified, the feelings can't help but give way.

To let pain in any form just sit around is disaster. If we don't get at it, we keep thinking about it. And the more we think about it, the more we emit those low vibratory frequencies to pull more pain to us. In other words, just to think about pain is to attract more, since what we focus on we draw to us, or become. But the moment we settle down and purposefully, deliberately ask for help in getting rid of the feelings, we immediately raise our frequency level, which in turn helps release the thought patterns which have been so securely stuck to our energy field.

Even if you're convinced right now that this pain of yours will never go, don't set limits on what your Inner Being can do for you. That's ego-thinking. Working with your Inner Being through prayer, meditation, or daily chats in the car can totally release hurt and pain from your life if you truly want it gone. But you might want to ask yourself if you're honestly ready to give up that comfortable identity of your outdated pain, which also means being its victim. Your answers may surprise you.

If you're truly ready to get rid of the habit, the only way to do it is to begin: (1) Pain comes, (2) *you feel it and experience it,* then

(3) you ask for help and let it go. Remember always, you are not pain; you only *think* you have it. So, watch how you react to it. With this "feel-and-release" formula, you begin to build a different power around you that changes the frequency in your energy field. The higher frequency cancels out the low.

Obviously, you can't just unthink something, but you can be powerfully aware in the moment of a new force beginning to work as you allow the pain to be experienced and then released. It's a matter of deciding in that moment, with the help of your Inner Being, that you're going to stay in the Now where the past can have no grip on you.

The fear of pain we're all running from, like scared rabbits, is a phantom! Absolutely the only place fear exists is in the intellectual thinking of the ego. The difficulty comes when we say we have no choice but to feel the pain. Ridiculous! It's that very thought that makes us so vulnerable, causing the pain to stay alive. Of course we have choices! They're limitless! Pain persists because of the *choice* we've made to retain it! So ask for help and watch what starts to happen. "From the Light of God that I am, I call forth help in removing my addiction to the pain of. . . ."

PROBLEMS: ANOTHER EGO FAVORITE

With some time on the Program, you undoubtedly have a basketful of former problems behind you. So why isn't there joy—I mean real joy—pouring forth in your life instead of, "Well, I guess this is it."

Whatever you've desired for your own kingdom, you've manifested—thought it into being—and that includes problems. Look around. Aren't the vast majority of us more concerned with our problems than we are with creating joy in our life? When was the last time you said to yourself, "Gee, I'd like to have a lot more joy today, and tomorrow, and the next day." Sure, uh-huh. But when was the last time you thought about a problem? Two minutes ago? Five seconds ago?

We're forever concentrating on what we don't want, like problems. You know by now what will happen, and it does. They stay all around us, magnetized to the hilt, drawn to us and around us as routinely as we pull the blankets over us at night.

If you're having problems with your kids, or your lover is making you unhappy, it's because you've allowed it. You've given them power over you. Spouse, boss, past, future, parents, bills—you've given your power away to anything outside of your own being that you allow to determine your reactions.

Predicaments, hang-ups, illnesses—they're all problems drawn *to* us, *by* us. We've thought them into being! Until we change the frequency of thinking that drew them to us in the first place, they'll stick to us like glue. Nor will ignoring a problem work, because the ego gets scared. Now we've got whatever that fear is sticking to us, holding the frequency of the problem in our energy field. The only way out of such a mess is to change the frequency that drew it to us in the first place.

STEPPING UP TO ANSWERS

If you're delighted with the idea of trying to solve problems day in and day out, go for it. If, however, you want to get them out of your life, the place to start is to pay attention to your thinking. Play with this exercise for, say, seven days. Take a particular problem you have in your life right now and tune in to how often it pops up in your thoughts throughout the day. What's the nature of your thinking surrounding this problem? Are your thoughts defensive against some other person, or blaming? If they are, you're seeing yourself as victim again and will continue to manifest that problem in your life until hell freezes over.

Throughout these seven days, as you become aware of how often you focus on your problem, remember that *how you think, you attract.* In other words, you can never find an answer by focusing on the problem. Instead, call the solution in by asking for it (even demanding it), which in turn will instantly raise your frequency and allow the answers to come. Raising your vibratory frequency to find your answers is the all-important step here, for you can never find the answer to a problem by staying in the same frequency in which you created it.

Ask for answers from within and from without. But ask! Ask every few minutes if you think of it, at work, in the car, making dinner. Talk to your Inner Being, talk to God, talk to the universe. Put out the call for help, and then do two things:

1) Leave the details of the answers up to your Inner Being, knowing with every fiber of your being those answers will come! Watch for them, listen for them, and stay out of your way, without trying to mastermind how the results are going to occur.

2) See yourself already living in the answer. In other words, you're reversing the Program expression, "Do the footwork, but don't plan the results." Now you're really planning the results, leaving the foot-work to your Inner Being.

Once you throw away the belief that solving problems is your life's work, and relax in the absolute knowledge that there are no problems you and your Inner Being can't solve, you'll be filled with such an elevated frequency it will be darn tough to remember the depth of pain the problem once caused.

When you go to sleep at night, suggest to your subconscious that solutions be given you in your sleep. This opens unbelievable doors, and it makes no difference if you remember your dreams or not. Remember, what you put out, you'll get back. So quit putting the low-frequency problems into your energy field and instead put out the high-frequency call for help. The answers to your problems will come as surely as light from the morning sun.

THE GREAT FEAR COVER-UP

One of the most amazing things about the ego is the manner in which it causes the mind to believe that it—the mind—is totally on its own, and that it alone must fight the lions in the jungle (which also, of course, implies there are lions to be fought!). The ego would have you think so, always.

When all that fear is frantically splashing around inside us, it's a sure sign we're attempting to trust in our own ego-strength. When was the last time you felt close to God when you were deep into fear? It can't happen. Fear is the most insidious of the ego cover-ups.

Like all our other limited thoughts, fear is only a state of mind, not a reality. Of course, we all know only too well that when we're in the midst of high emotional fear, it most assuredly does feel like a reality, and we struggle with everything in our ego-selves not to crumble under its awesome weight.

But fear is just a fungus! Let it grow, and it will kill you. It may kill you from early old age, pneumonia, drugs, or hiccups, but it'll kill you. Like any other negative emotion that comes from the ego, fear is a disbelief in ourselves. The only true healing we have, be it physical, emotional, intellectual, or spiritual, is the release from fear.

No doors are more powerful in closing off the Light to our Inner Being than those of fear. When we're afraid of anything, we give it power to hurt us and permission to grow and spread. Depression, anxiety, resentment, greed, anger, jealousy, doubt, hatred—all have their roots in the ego's twisted logic of fear.

So what's the answer? Can we really live without fear? Of course we can. Fear is just an appeal for help, so call on your whole being to address this challenge for as long as it takes. Mastery, after all, is a way of life, an ongoing daily process in which you address each fear, no matter how small, as it comes into your thoughts.

THE DEATH OF FEAR

The first thing to do when you experience that old familiar feeling is to identify the actual area of your body where you feel it. You'll almost always spot it in a particular area, such as your stomach, or throat. The purpose of this exercise is for you to see that the feeling is *only in that area* and not throughout your entire being. You are not fear, you are *having it*, like a bad piece of meat, but it's still your choice to have it. (Then you might ask yourself why on Earth you'd want to have a bad piece of meat anyhow.)

Next, once you've located the fear-point in your body, call on your Inner Being to help you ask the fear what it's trying to tell you. Actually challenge it, speak to it, and go into it. As you do, you begin to see it's nothing more than an empty room you've been carefully avoiding. Call to the God of your Being for assistance and walk inside. Face the bloody thing! It's not a monstrous enemy. It's an energy that can be your teacher if you'll just call forth the courage to face it. Avoid it, and its power magnifies.

Your fear wants something from you, so find out what that something is. Say to it (even if you're curled up against the wall in panic, as I once was), "My friend, I know you're here, and I remember you only too well. I know you've come to remind me of something I've forgotten. Come and sit with me and the God of my Being so that we can remember together." Now here's where your new Mastery really comes into play; you begin to see your fears as lessons rather than tortures.

Continue to speak to the fear as a parent would speak to an injured child, wrapping it with love and tenderness, for that low frequency of emotion cannot possibly exist in the high frequency of love and compassion. One overrides the other, and soon the death of that fear will be certain. But you have to take control; fear can never be just wished away.

Fear, pain, anger, hate, jealousy, problems, loneliness, whatever; if we want to walk this path back to our true identity, our Godhood, those ego-image onionskins need to get peeled off. We created them all to fill a void, a hole in our gut that we didn't understand, so we filled it with fear. There was an emptiness in our soul, so we filled it with pain.

We can get rid of those monsters, because they're not real; they're our ego's games we allowed over the years to deny our own identity. They are, in the final understanding, the games we've created to deny God. So fasten your seat belt, because any thought you may have of exposing this cover-up of your real Self will probably create a mighty (and fearful) stir from your ego. Like, yeowww!! That's OK. It's just terrified of the newness. Simply love it, give it a chance to get used to the new territory, and you'll have an ally for life.

Which teacher do you want to follow? Old thinking or new, ego-self or God-self, the choice is yours. When pain comes, or fear, or problems, stop and ask yourself that very question. And then remember from the depths of your being, "My life is mine, and I form it!"

CHAPTER 8
BELIEF CREATES YOUR REALITY

Without question, subconscious beliefs are the singular most powerful force within us responsible for the creation of our private worlds. Beliefs, remember, are thoughts, so if you really believe a thing, you have strong emotional thought working around it, and the effect will follow, whether you are consciously thinking it or not. Belief creates experience!

There are two basic kinds of beliefs; first are the core beliefs. These are somewhat universal in nature, such as "mankind is inherently bad" or "you have to compromise to get along in this world." We build our lives around core beliefs, and, while we're usually aware of them, they're not something we focus on to any great degree. But core beliefs are intensely strong electromagnetically and will easily attract experiences to which they're magnetically aligned.

Second are the personal beliefs pertaining, as the name implies, to the self. "I'm afraid of people." "My life is worthless." "I'm easy to please." "I hate doctors." All beliefs we hold about ourselves fall into this group, including our identities.

Actually, any idea we accept as true becomes a belief we hold on to, either consciously or subconsciously. And there's not a belief we have that could be considered useless. They're all as alive and active in us as spitting cobras, only much more deadly.

Granted, many of our earliest beliefs were not of our own making, coming from family, church, and all manner of places outside of us. Because of this early and unconscious acceptance by us of what others considered to be true, it would be ludicrous to categorically state there are no such things as victims, for until we know that thought creates reality, we're victims to our lack of knowledge. Look at all those belief systems handed down from generation to generation that perpetuate cultural idiosyncrasies. And we're certainly all aware of the mountain of beliefs originating in our childhood. Any of these scenarios might understandably cause us to react as victims.

Most of our beliefs are stuffed. If, for instance, abuse or unhappy circumstances were part of our childhood, we tend to categorize the feelings associated with those beliefs as dangerous, so we do what we consider to be safe and put them away. This, of course, is about the worst thing we can do. Those ignored beliefs sit in our subconscious as expectancies, ready to generate a fear of any feelings associated with them. We don't want to feel 'em, so we hide 'em, and whammo! The power of attraction is increased tenfold by the stuffing. Those beliefs now become our reality.

BELIEFS ARE NOT FACTS

The key to changing a belief is to understand that it's the belief that's the culprit, not the emotion it generates! In other words, we're terrified of the emotion, of the feeling related to the thought of a past event, not of the belief itself. Once we get at the belief, the fearful emotion associated with it will vanish.

The trouble comes in our chronic habit of concentrating on what we want to avoid! If you're afraid of spiders, and there's a little guy crawling around your ceiling, it's going to be pretty hard for you to take your eyes off it out of fear it will fall on you. The same is true with our beliefs from the past. We concentrate on them, consciously or otherwise, and in that concentration draw to us more and more of what we're trying to avoid, the emotions of the belief. "My dad was awful when he was drunk." "My mom didn't like me." "I was always so alone." "I'll never get over being raped." Just think those old beliefs and, in a flash, their painful emotions follow.

The challenge now is to get our outdated beliefs unstuffed so we can clear our energy field. For one last time, then, or perhaps for the first time, we reach down and make ourselves *feel* what we've been so long avoiding, to begin the process of release.

Feelings, remember, are not facts! Just because you allow yourself to feel them does not mean they are true! But until you allow yourself the experience of the feeling, it will stay with you forever and a day. Deny the emotion that goes with the belief, or pretend it away, and you keep the lid on the belief itself. You'll never be able to question it or take it apart and blow it away. You've got to get in there and dig out the belief in back of the emotion before the emotion can be cut loose and released.

We're not at the mercy of our childhood beliefs any more than we're at the mercy of our present-day beliefs, unless we believe we are. But our imagination follows our beliefs and is forever painting these horror pictures in our mind's eye about our fears and lacks.

That just sends in the reinforcements to keep those negative beliefs alive. All you have to remember is that what you're working with are only beliefs! That's all they are. They are not real! *They are not facts.*

Maybe this will help. Think of beliefs as pieces of furniture in your living room. Some of it's old and outdated, ready for Goodwill. Some pieces are perhaps worn, but comfortable, though you might like to spruce them up a bit. Either way, you need to clean house and rearrange to get ready for the new.

So it becomes a process of identifying the beliefs we want to clean out. When you've got one isolated and are ready to get rid of it, step back and say, "OK, this is not necessarily true, even though I used to believe it, so it can go. Now!" But just as we've said on the Program from day one, you can't take something away without replacing it with something else. Take that old belief away, and it creates a void ready to be filled with a new belief. Now it's time to reprogram with the help of your Inner Being.

REPROGRAMMING YOUR BELIEFS

If your life at present is not following your desires, it's being dutifully guided by your beliefs, both those that you're aware of and those that are deeply hidden. Obviously, to attempt to dig up and take an inventory of every belief you hold would entail a task of monumental proportions. While such infinite detail is not necessary (and frankly impossible), most of the major beliefs currently running your life can easily be found, addressed, and either saved or reprogrammed according to the importance you award them.

Part One is the inventory.

One of the simplest and most immediately rewarding methods of reprogramming unwanted beliefs is to match the belief to the problem it's causing in your life and then to reverse the process by matching a particular problem with the belief that has caused it. And what makes this exercise even more fun is that you can start at either end, so to speak, with either problems or beliefs, whichever seems easiest for you.

If you begin with beliefs you want to uncover, you'll need two pages, one for "core beliefs" and the other for "personal beliefs." Head the upper left of the first paper with Core Beliefs and the upper right with Problem Caused, drawing a line down the center of the paper. Now list all the major core beliefs (remember, these are of a universal nature) you can think of on the left of the page (i.e., "Men get better jobs than women") and on the right half, the problem it has caused in your life, if indeed there's been a problem (i.e., "As a woman, I find it difficult to get top executive jobs").

Do the same on paper with Personal Beliefs. You'll find this page rolls out rather rapidly, along with Problems Caused. You may find a number of hidden surprises as you get into the swing of it.

After you've taken a stab at that with both core and personal beliefs, turn it around and now head the upper left of a page with Current Problems. Draw your line down the middle, and on the top right list Operant Belief. This right side will now be a mixture of core and personal, so there's no need to separate them. Begin with the major problems as you perceive them to be in your life at present, and then pull up the belief system that's in back of it. By reversing the process in this manner, you'll find innumerable beliefs you weren't aware of, or didn't uncover in the first exercise.

Part Two is reprogramming.

Remembering that any belief, no matter its nature, is only an idea *about* reality and not reality itself, we come now to a superb technique for replacing the unwanted *old* with the desired *new*.

First, using your divine imagination to take you back, generate the *feelings* which go with the old belief you want to replace. Do this only once. Though it may be unpleasant, let those feelings come through, even if only for a few moments.

If, for example, you have a belief of being shy, jump into that feeling feetfirst, getting into all its feelings of insecurity, fear, etc. Or, if you believe your days are meaningless, really get into the feelings of loneliness, or self-pity, or worthlessness.

Now, turn your imagination all the way around and let the exact opposite of those feelings flow through you. What you're doing is allowing your imagination (the God of you) to forcibly create the emotions you want. So, your feelings of shyness deliberately flow into grand feelings of confidence, being gregarious, being carefree. Your feelings of pointlessness flow into deliberate days of fulfillment, or feelings of joy and contentment, however you want to create the reverse scenario through your unlimited imagination. As you experience the emotional joy of these new beliefs, they're imprinting new programming on your subconscious, putting new expectancies into your energy field, overriding the old with the higher frequencies of unlimitedness.

Now back that up with repeated visualization and deliberate pretense. In visualizing this new you, see yourself for five minutes each day in this new role. See the people about you responding in a different manner than ever before. This will actually set new thought patterns about those people which will, in turn, begin to alter their old reactions to you.

Then put the old Program adage into use by "pretending as if." For a few minutes each day, talk about your new belief out loud to yourself just as if you were chatting with a friend. "Honestly, Sam, I love this new way of thinking because . . ." You're focusing on the present, securing the new belief in place until it becomes operational and permanent.

We're all used to taking inventories. If you'll approach this reprogramming with the same fervent desire you did with your Program inventory, the results will astound you. Call Home to your Inner Being for help before you begin the process, and you'll be amazed at how easily the old beliefs and their attendant problems will unfold to be released. You'll also be amazed at how easily your imagination, fired by intention, conjures up the desired new feelings through highly creative images and vastly expanded thoughts.

Part Three is releasing uncovered beliefs.

This is far and away the easiest of the reprogramming exercises, for it involves nothing but a few moments of thought daily.

Calling on your Inner Being, you simply release all beliefs which no longer serve you, and do this in the form of a blanket affirmation, or prayer, whether or not you know what those beliefs may be. While this is not a substitute for the important physical and emotional activities involved in Parts One and Two, it will ultimately release those deeply hidden beliefs of which we're not aware, the kinds that so strongly affect our lives in ways we can't conceive because of their enormous emotional power.

"I willingly release all beliefs that no longer
lovingly serve me, and I choose love
in all areas of my life. So be it!"

You've made the affirmation here of willingness, a vital step in release. Next, you've identified your desire for the energy of love to manifest in your life. By making this blanket prayer, or affirmation, a part of your daily life, you automatically begin the process of releasing and reprogramming on both conscious and unconscious levels. Remember to call Home for help and let the power that you are surround and support you every step of the way.

MELTING OLD BELIEFS

Very few of us have ever known, seen, felt, or even believed how incomprehensibly loved we are by the God of our being. All of our lives we've looked outside ourselves to fill that gnawing hunger within. Of course that never worked, because what we're looking for is right within us. It's what we're made of, or what we are.

Granted, the power of this highest of frequencies we call love is beyond our current ability to comprehend. Yet give that power freedom, and it rapidly begins melting away those damnable ego needs and useless beliefs which have held us in such bondage most of our lives.

Remember our two teachers? What is not coming through as God in us is ego. Or, put another way, whatever is not activated in us as love is fear in one form or another, and that includes all those beliefs which no longer serve us.

It's important we remember that this force of love within us doesn't have to be manufactured; it's already there! All we have to do is pull it back up into our awareness, and instantly the process of transformation is begun. We're simply practicing getting back in touch with what we are, getting rid of unwanted ego habits in the process.

There is a powerful, yet incredibly simple, way to activate this energy. The process is so simple, one might think it has no effect. Yet if you remembered nothing else from this book but these three words and used them faithfully throughout your day, everything in your life would change. Those words are:

"I choose love!"

How could the speaking, or thinking, of that little phrase possibly change your life? How does one just decide to *choose love* when most of us haven't the foggiest idea what that means, much less know how? And there we go again, with questions of disbelief and defiance popping up from the ego with its familiar "prove it" attitude.

The fact is, we don't need to know how it works, nor do we need to know how to do it. Our Inner Being knows precisely what that statement means and expands its energy in the moment of the thought to meet whatever situation is at hand.

For example, you become aware of one of your old beliefs in operation. "I choose love." That's all you have to say with conviction and belief, and the melting begins.

You're facing a difficult time at work. "I choose love." You have a resentment or some other attitude going you want to get rid of, or bills you can't pay. You have a desire to change jobs or take a trip; you want happiness, or peace, or health in your life; you want to stop your anger or learn to like your mother-in-law; "I choose love."

On the freeway, in the shower, over the stove, at meetings, mowing the lawn, speak these words from the depth of your being, feel their reality, believing what you're saying with everything in you. The God you are will do the rest. "I choose love," the most powerful three words you could ever believe!

RING OF ICE, FIRE OF LOVE

Every time we dissolve some aspect of our negative ego, our Inner Being is able to shine through a little brighter to attract more positive happenings into our lives. If we hold tightly to our fearful old beliefs and anxieties, though, there's no way that Light—our high-frequency primal energy we call love—can get through.

One of the most helpful formulas I've found for releasing that inner core of love came from a dear friend who was assisting at a seminar. Since this was Sandy's first visit to our town, I agreed to go, though I could think of forty-three other things I'd rather have done that weekend. The subject matter left me cold, but I thought, "What the heck; maybe I'll get something out of it." And anyhow, I didn't want to let my old friend down.

I might have known what was going on. Talk about being in the right place at the right time! The God of my being had kicked me right in the you-know-what and said, "Go! There's something important for you to learn." Sandy's little story took hold of my mind and offered one of the most exciting ways I've found to melt away the ego's tough walls. I've used it almost daily since that weekend, and the changes that have ensued are beyond measure. The story that follows begins with our first cries for air.

When we come into this world we bring with us, in the center of our being, the undivided purity of Isness, our Light, the real core of all that we are. That force, which we'll call the Is, being the God essence and therefore creative, wants to expand as does all con- sciousness. So, from the time of Its birth in bodily form, It employs the process of cause and effect. It learns to walk. It bumps into a tree two or three times and finally realizes there may be another way to go. Next time, It goes around the tree. Thus comes learning, and with each learning comes an expansion of the Is, an actual expansion of Light within the physical body.

Like the youngster learning of its new world, the Isness grows with each learning. But something happens. A decree comes down from an outside authority (maybe a parent) that for some reason or other it's "wrong" to go around that tree. So the Is, which once found pleasure in going around the tree, is now confused. Because "wrong" is not yet a part of Its learning, the Is continues to go around the tree, but in the process begins to identify Its action of going around the tree as "wrong." Thus, the first negative cube of ice forms on the outer Ring of Self. The outer ring, once known to the Is as pure personality ego, has been altered by a negative feeling of guilt.

As time goes on, more programming comes to the Is, more "should's" and "do's" and "don'ts." What was once simple cause and effect becomes a complex, confusing set of procedures.

The beliefs of "should's," "do's," and "don'ts" increase, and so do the negative cubes of ice on the once-pure ring of the outer-self. Ice cubes of fear, anxiety, caution, confusion, need, and survival are added to the first cube of guilt already frozen firmly in place. Finally, a whole shell of ice cubes forms a tight ring about the Is, walling in the once-clear outer ego-ring. The Is finds Itself held prisoner by the thickening walls of Its own limitations with no apparent way out. As the Ring of Ice from the now-altered ego grows and grows, the Is becomes more subdued, enslaved by Its own free will, unable to live in Its own Light.

Now the Is has a real problem. Its job is to light the path for Its physical being, but not only is It increasingly ignored by Its physical being, Its Light and energy are becoming dimmer and dimmer with each new cube that's added.

Never asleep, the Is has an idea. Since the circular wall is made of ice cubes, and since the Is was made of the Fire of Love, It decides to go after the cubes by melting them, one at a time. Each time It dissolves a cube, the Is reasons, It will have room to expand Its Fire of Love that much more! Wonderful!

With much excitement, the Is begins this hopeful new task of breaking out. Every day It finds some little, altered-ego cube to dissolve with Its fire and quickly expands Its Love to fill the space. Because It wants out more than anything in the whole universe, never a day goes by without at least one cube being dissolved. So never a day goes by without Its love expanding.

Slowly at times with little cubes, and more rapidly with bigger cubes, the melting continues, and the Is expands Its central Fire of Love. It doesn't matter to the Is how slow or fast the process, as long as It can melt at least one or two of the cubes each day.

Then it happens. One day, more glorious than angels have words to describe, the Is has so diminished the cubes of altered ego that there's an actual hole in the Ring! Without a second thought, the Is expands Itself to the very reaches of Its endurance, right out into the great beyond. The Is has returned Home, Its long journey complete. It has expanded Itself back to Itself. It has gone back to Its original Light, the All In All, the Source, the God, the original Is from whence it came.

Now, this little story may not be worthy of a Hemingway or Hans Christian Andersen, but it's played a major part in allowing me to feel and expand the love around which I'm built, my God-self.

Find time to acknowledge your Is (your Inner Being) each day, asking It to create some small altered-ego happening to dissolve. Maybe the cube, in the form of "image," is nothing more than going downtown without makeup, or going without the usual tie to your formal meeting, wonderful examples of old belief systems. Whatever it is, as soon as you do it, actually see a cube melted on your altered-ego Ring of Ice, and let the feeling of the expansion of love within you become real. Don't just think you feel that expansion within. Make yourself feel it!

Visualize your own Is as a power of fiery love within you, long, long overdue for release. Feel It there, wanting to awaken, wanting to come out. Then simply stay alert throughout your day for opportunities to melt, for instance, a cube of blame (we've got lots of those), or a cube of an old belief, or a cube of criticism or judgment (actually, they're all beliefs). We all have more than enough cubes of "should's" or "can'ts" (also old belief systems). If it's any kind of limited thinking, it's an old belief system in operation, and it belongs in the altered-ego Ring of Ice to be melted.

One day you may find yourself saying an unaccustomed "No" to a request. A cube melted! Or perhaps you hold your tongue from verbal judgment against someone. A cube melted. Then perhaps you make a decision to feel love for that same person, in addition to withholding judgment. A big cube melted. You ask for help in solving an "unsolvable" problem. A bigger cube melted. The next day you take responsibility for having gotten yourself into a situation without blaming anyone; wow, a huge cube melted, while the fiery core of love within you is having more and more room in which to expand.

You can have wonderfully tangible results with this process. You're staying in the Now, your negativity is turning around, and you're beginning to trust your Inner Being. You're practicing pulling up and feeling the love you are. Find some ice cube of belief to melt every day, and just the shift in focus will raise your frequency.

Changes start gradually, then begin to snowball. As you remove each altered-ego limitation, you feel more secure, more sure of yourself. Your fears begin to melt. Shadows of your past lose their stranglehold. You take back more power. People, places, and things no longer own you. Life is no longer lonely, and you're being filled with the exquisite beauty of the Now. Above all, there's love in your life, the wondrous, intoxicating love of you.

So allow those old, unwanted beliefs and limitations to unfold in all their glory, no matter how distasteful they may be to reexperience. Bless them, and be grateful they're coming into your awareness. That's loving them, and they simply cannot survive on love!

Above all, don't let yourself be held back by what you think is the enormity of your outdated beliefs. Walk on, don't stop. As happened when we came to the Program, in the walking comes the courage, the experience, and the trust that transcends thought. In that place, no one or no thing can turn you back, no matter how difficult the circumstances may seem at the time.

Once you give that Isness in you Its head, and let Its Light expand to melt the ego identity, you come into harmony with You, in harmony with life. You'll know where you're going and why, because you'll know who's in control.

"From the Light of God that I am, I *willingly* release all old beliefs that no longer serve me. And I choose love in all areas of my life. So be it!"

CHAPTER 9
RESTRUCTURING THE PAST

The first stages of getting our lives turned around are the most simple—and the most difficult—for, like our Twelve-Step Program, they require choice and surrender. Early on we acknowledge a lack of understanding as to what we really are but are willing to dig to whatever depths necessary to find out, and so begin our journey back to remembrance.

In truth, the process of that digging can be painful if approached from the vantage of ego. God knows, we've all had our fill of inventories and soul searching. "Enough, we say. No more, I've had enough." And I'd be the first one to agree. If wallowing endlessly in all that old emotional gunk is what's necessary to reignite our Godhood, then most of us would probably say, "Thank you very much, but I'll see ya!"

Happily, there is "an easier, softer way," and it's called the magnetism of desire. If your aim in reading this book is to think about doing a little bit of changing, or seeing if there's anything in here that will *fix* your life and all its worries right now, that's OK. It's a start, just like coming to the Program because you thought it might help you *handle* your addiction. Of course, if a little bit is what you're after, a little bit is what you'll get.

On the other hand, if you fan that desire with a passion to move from fear to truth, so be it; you will. If your passionate desire is to become Master rather than victim, you will, all the way to the Light of God that you are (which, after all, is what we came here to do). What brings it about is a deliberate calling forth of our divine will known as desire, *with the proviso that all lessons, all awakenings, be brought forth in peace.* It works. You've now ignited the fuel to restructure your life without the fear of getting stuck, once again, in all of that old pain.

THE CALL OF DESIRE

Desire (passionate will) is a powerful magnetic energy, the essence of which is love. But no desire, no magnetism. And yes, desire *can* be created.

Although we may not have known until now the enormity of our divine powers, we've certainly been powerful enough to create our own lack. Now, as in Step Three, we make another conscious decision, this time to use that awesome power to create freedom. Indeed, it's on wings of passion born of desire that we fly Home.

The process begins, once again, with our old friend the pituitary. Just as the pituitary controls the degree to which our brains are open, desire literally controls the opening of its seal. By the simple but sincere act of going inside and calling forth desire, we're alerting our Inner Being which, in turn, nudges our frequency to a slightly higher range, which then tickles the pituitary's seal into opening a wee bit wider. All this from desire. Of course, the more passionate the desire, the quicker the opening.

"From the Light of God that I am, I call forth desire to know. So be it."

"From the Light of God that I am, I call forth desire to understand. So be it."

Call it forth every day until you know it's made a permanent home in your subconscious. "From the Light of God that I am, I call forth the awareness of desire to be ever present in my reality. So be it."

Being, or all of what we are, is both electric (meaning it transmits) and magnetic (meaning it pulls in). It's a force field of tremendous cosmic power evolving toward God-self awareness. By igniting that central core of energy with passionate desire, we're magnetizing everything in and about us to wake up, now!

So you decide to try this thing, because you really want it. You sneak quietly into the bathroom, lock the door, get into the shower where you're sure you're safe from other eyes and ears, and tentatively call forth your desire "from the Light of God" that you are. Doesn't seem so bad. You try it again, this time with more gusto. Feels OK. But now the third time you really get into it, you feel the want, you feel the desire, and you call it forth with a fervor that reaches down to your very core. Hello! You've just called Home, and the call has been received, loud and clear.

Instantly everything in you begins heating up like an old steam engine getting shoveled full of coal. Your chemistry changes in that very moment, and the energy starts its first chug, chug, chug into permanent residence in your subconscious. New vibrations go zipping out, searching for experiences to match the newly created frequencies, all because you reached for higher thought, *the desire to know.* Now watch the impact. If you'll keep at it until the desire is firm within you (and you'll know), different people will be drawn to you to offer new experiences, you'll find a particular book with meaningful teachings, a speaker at a meeting will say something significant, someone special will call, you'll feel a need to watch a certain TV show, you'll start to get intuitive thoughts to do this, or go there, or call them—changes, teachings, lessons, offerings.

But are they coincidences? No! Your raised vibrations are going out to begin their grand search, backed by the power of the universe which you called forth on your own through desire. I can tell you from firsthand experience that once you put in the call, your desire (and the changes it brings to your life) will never cease.

The day was freezing, but my tears were hot and plentiful. I had just finished a seminar session with my favorite spiritual teacher and was overcome with feelings of love and awe for my reality. But would those feelings last? Or more important, how could I make them last?

I made a beeline for my special meadow where I could sit beneath a great fir to drink in heady views of the Continental Divide. Colorado in May is pure splendor. I asked my Inner Being what to do. How could I make sure the deep desire I was experiencing in that moment would remain? I wanted to stay on this path, but what would ensure me against ego sabotage and a voice I didn't want to hear saying, "Oh, to hell with it! This is just too damn much trouble." Almost instantly an inner voice broke into my thoughts. "You know what to do, Lynn; ask! Nothing happens until you ask, remember? Call forth your desire, and call it forth in peace."

Ask for desire? Well, OK, why not! So I did. From the depths of my being I put in a call: "From the Light of God that I am, I call forth the desire to remain on my path and that my lessons and teachings come only in peace." The tears started. "And I call it forth on a daily basis." But I wanted all bases covered. "And if for any reason the desire should lessen" (tears were all over the place), "send me the desire to create the desire!" The cosmic realms were undoubtedly rolling in stitches of loving laughter, but I had never been more serious.

Since my fervent call from the snowy mountains, that burning desire has only grown stronger. Whenever I've felt like saying "nuts," something has always come to turn that feeling around. So all I can say is, if you want it, if you want that desire to create a brilliant magnetic force field around you to keep you focused in this process of awakening into your Godhood, just put in the call, and so it will be.

Then look out! Once you've called forth your desire to awaken with deep sincerity, you've now consciously asked your soul to begin a recharting of your life's course. Since it already knows where the greatest amount of resistance is on this long-awaited route, it's not going to waste any time in showing it to you, and the road may get bumpier than you had bargained for. So don't forget to call forth that your journey be in peace! Then let it come, whether there's still some pain in the bumps or not. The pain's not going to last forever, and *this will be your last time through it.*

When you were a youngster, did you ever have a bad fall off a bicycle and have to go to the doctor to clean out all the stones and tar embedded in one whole side of you that was scraped to a dirty pulp? Nothing broken, just those painful scrapes that needed cleaning before you could begin to heal. So you went for help.

We're doing the same thing here. Sometimes it isn't so pleasant, but that's OK; we've been here before and made it. We can surely make it now when our very essence is at stake, not to mention our lives. Just keep calling forth the desire for more knowingness, more

understanding, and more realization of your true self. Calling for
that Light of desire is what creates the healing.

THE NECESSITY OF OWNING IT ALL

Now comes the Number One lesson: *we can't change anything
in our lives until we accept that we've created all of it.* So here we
are, living in these manufactured identities which are nothing more
than the shells under which we've hidden our lifelong pain. If we're
"willing to go to any lengths," to walk out of our victimhood of discomfort into mastery of our destiny, then we're ready to say, "Bring
it on; whatever it is, bring it on." While we call forth in peace whatever is needed for us to learn, we can turn away from nothing.
Absolutely nothing!

To face everything in our known past and call forward all that's
still hidden from us, regardless of how dark and dismal it may seem,
takes a mighty, mighty decision. However, once that decision is
made, there comes a deep resolve to face whatever may be uncovered, no matter the fear of pain. In other words, no turning our
backs on anything that comes. We face it, and we own it.

*The beauty of owning anything is
that once we own it, we never have
to experience it again . . . ever.*

So what does it mean "to own"? Owning is admitting, taking
responsibility, opening all doors, not denying, releasing, then allowing the event or emotion to become wisdom rather than jailer.
Owning means walking right into the emotion, or addiction, or

problem, and claiming it as our own creation. It means letting it resonate through every cell in our being, with whatever pain that may entail, to come to that point of surrender where we can finally, and forever, give it up.

Owning means releasing through acceptance, love, and forgiveness of ourselves whatever we've done, thought, or created in our past. It does not mean trying to release by rejecting that past, for what is rejected (stuffed) can never be released.

Owning is taking responsibility for our emotions without blame. It's saying, for instance, "I alone created the emotion of hate against my mother, she didn't. She may have been the fuel, but I lit the match. No one held a gun to my head and told me I had to hate her all my life in order to have someone to blame for my self-imposed pain." Once we own that emotion as our own creation, it no longer owns us. It becomes a "no-thing" in our lives, for the energy of that magnetic thought is released from our energy field and no longer rules our lives.

No Regrets!

How often do we look back with regret at certain events we've created in our lives, such as "failed" relationships or businesses, things we've said or done, all those grand "mistakes" we think we've made along the way? We speak of the need to stop blaming others in order to get out of pain, problems, and victimhood, but what about blaming ourselves? Is there really any difference? Absolutely not!

Looking without regret—*without regret*—at anything we've done or felt, past or present, is our first leg up to self-acceptance. It's a vital step, for as long we persist in blaming ourselves for past actions or thoughts, no matter how small or inconsequential, those thoughts remain, magnetizing unwanted events, and blocking any hope of higher frequency thought.

There is absolutely nothing in the human experience more insidiously destructive than self-judgment. In the teachings of every great master, judgment of self is categorically labeled as the single most destructive impediment to self-empowerment. At the very least, it is probably the surest way in the world to keep us stuck in lack of self-acceptance, or love of self.

So look within at your life, all those little secrets you hate to think about, all the things you wish you'd done differently. Feel them, allow them, then own them. Once and for all, stop blaming yourself and realize that you did what you did for the adventure and wisdom of the experience. You no longer need to be crippled by that event or emotion for the rest of your life. Own it now, and let it go with no regrets so it will no longer own you.

From the Light of God that you are, call forth every hurt, every deception, every sorrow, everything that's still an open sore. Examine each one and allow yourself to feel each one, one at a time. Then, "From the Light of God that I am, I forgive myself for having created you; I embrace you, I love you, and I release you to become wisdom in my soul rather than jailer of my being." Say it out loud. Speak to the emotion, the hurt, or the shame. Love it. Then, like the oyster who embraces the painful grain of sand into its being, own it, and allow it to form into a lustrous, highly valued pearl of wisdom. And always remember, *you will never again have to experience what you have owned.*

On the other hand, we do have free will, and if you should have a yen for keeping up the self-pity of past "mistakes," well, go for it! Just be aware of your choice and realize you're doing it *because you want to*, not because "you can't help it."

"From the Light of God that I am, I call forth my willingness to accept all I have done and felt in my life, without regret. So be it."

That's an Option

How many times during the day do we have a thought of self-recrimination, judging ourselves unmercifully for this-or-that action, this-or-that thought? Some of the thoughts may seem innocent enough, like a fleeting doubt of our capabilities, or persistent feelings of insecurity. "I doubt I'll ever be able to change my thinking." "I feel silly saying I'm God." "I don't have anything to say at meetings." "I don't like myself much today." These are all choices we make in the moment to keep ourselves stuck in limited thinking.

One of the most productive—and truly fun—ways to view the process of *owning* is to see it from the vantage of *choice*. As you become more and more aware of your thoughts and how limiting they are, in that moment of awareness, stop and say to yourself, "Well, that's an option," and change the thought! By doing that, you've owned the feeling behind the thought in that instant, and released it from your energy field. As any routine thought pops into your head which you view as limited, or self-judging, absolutely insist on giving yourself the choice of whether you really want to think it into being or not. "Well, that's an option!"

In some cases you may want to go ahead with the feeling and will choose not to change it for the moment so it can be felt and released. Perhaps it's an "ugly" sexual fantasy, or feeling of enormous hostility, even a desire to murder. Embrace it! Allow it to be a conscious part of you, love it as your own creation, forgive it, and release it to become wisdom. "Yes, I used to think that . . ." Then it's finished!

Owning means looking at all our limited feelings, whatever is still controlling us from our past, and turning those feelings around to embrace as our own choiceful creations. It means when we run up against jealousy, or envy, or anger, or self-doubt, we take instant control of our thoughts, making a decision in the moment whether to pursue that line of thinking or not.

"Yes, I used to think that . . ." Then if all else fails, and you can't decide in that instant how to change the thought, go for the choice of love. A thought comes, and you recognize its intent as limited ego thinking. "Yes, I used to think . . ." Or, "Well, that's an option, and instead I choose love." That's all. It's so simple.

RELEASING THE BLAMES

Nature in any form is a grand healer because of its high frequencies. One of the gentlest ways I've found to release my blames or "if only's" (the ones we made in the first chapter) is to take them to a quiet place in the out-of-doors, a place where I can be absolutely alone. When you're set and settled, go inside to that still, quiet place of your Inner Being. Speak from the Light of the God that you are and ask your Inner Being to surround you in its frequency of love, asking it over and over until you actually feel the connection. Perhaps it will be a tingling in your head or hands. Perhaps it will be a feeling of great peace, or safety, or joy. If tears come, allow them. In that connection, you're feeling, for perhaps the first time in your life, the love you've always wanted and never knew was available.

Now speak from the Light of the God that you are and ask your Inner Being to help you release all the old blames and resentments. Speak them out loud, one by one. "From the Light of God that I am, I call forth release of my resentment against . . ." By this simple statement, you're calling forth forgiveness and transmuting in the frequency of love all that's been clouding your life in blame. Then finally, speak to your Inner Being and ask for help in owning all that's on your list. "From the Light of God that I am, I call forth ownership of all that I have been, all that I am, and all that I have created."

It takes courage to go out by yourself and begin the process of loving who and what you are. When you can call in all your perceived mistakes, or blames, or resentments, and really get in touch with that desire to accept the fact that you created them all; when you can look at yourself and your life and say, "I am unhappy because I made myself that way"; when you know everything in your life is a result of your attitudes, and that if you're miserable it's because you made yourself miserable; and when you can honestly look at every little activity in your past or daily life and see how much of a victim you've allowed yourself to be, and own it all, then you begin to feel a refreshing, cleansing joy. You feel a closeness, a reverence, and an indescribable feeling of gratitude. It's the God you are saying, "Hello there, Little One. Good for you! Welcome to your journey Home."

DUMPING THE PAST

In our recovery programs we take an inventory of our past actions, talk them over with our sponsor, or some other human being, and our Higher Power. Then we make a list of all the people we've harmed and make amends. These are empowering steps from our Program. Hopefully, once out in the open, we find the strength to forgive ourselves.

But what about the people who "did it" to us that didn't go down on our lists? How do you find the power to release them? How do you own the hate toward a family member who molested you, hate that reaches to your very core? How do you own your despising of the father who left you, the mother who beat you, or the parents who overindulged you?

Difficult as it may be to accept, and cruel as it may be to hear, the only reason those feelings are still with us is because, like our thoughts, we've chosen to have them. The cold hard truth is, if we don't like what we're feeling, we, and we alone, are the only ones who can change it, not Uncle John, Mom or Dad, or any other ghost from our past. It's our creation, therefore our choice to stop the hurting, not theirs.

Whenever a feeling comes over you that says you have no choice whether to feel it or not, stop the world, and do the same with the feeling that you did with a thought. "Well, that's an option. I can decide to have the feeling or not."

You can make a choice whether to feel a feeling or not. The need to feel that old pain is nothing but a trick your ego is playing on you to avoid assuming the responsibility for, and therefore the joy of, life. You're an unlimited being of Light. Take control! Recognize what's happening and don't let your ego have its way.

We can create for ourselves intolerable suffering if we still believe it's necessary, but it's not necessary. In fact, the thought that we're choiceless regarding the hold the past has over us is what makes us so vulnerable, so afraid of even thinking about it.

Remember, it wasn't the events that undermined us, but our responses to them. The event is long gone. Why are we hanging on to our old reactions?

Our Big Book says, "We stopped fighting every thing and every body." Once we say, "Enough! I'm an unlimited God, and I choose to take control of my thoughts," we've finally stopped fighting our ghosts. More important, we've stopped fighting ourselves. We've owned our past and released the electromagnetic thoughts which have continued to attract the same events into our world.

Bear in mind, though, that owning the past is quite different from wishing it away, for *wishing* only serves to stuff the feelings rather than experience them for release and ultimate ownership. So allow the pain to come forward. See it as part of all that has formed you, own it, and polish it into wisdom.

Now, what about the people in your past who "did" all those things? There are a lot of books out that say "love 'em." Well, if you can figure out a way to do that, more power to you! To me, that's like trying to swim upstream with one-hundred-pound weights on both feet. By trying to love *those* people from our past, we're still wanting from them what we want for ourselves, i.e., love, approval, etc. We're trying to give away what we want to keep for ourselves to someone we don't even like, much less love. Then we feel guilty because we can't accomplish something we think we *should*. Whew! Sound familiar?

So, rather than struggling to love the people, love the *feelings* you have for them, no matter how vile those feelings may seem. The feelings, remember, are your own creations. Once you recognize and accept that, you can own them.

Keep it simple. Just love your feelings about the troublesome people in your past, no matter what those feelings may be. Then love yourself for not loving them, be they family, or friends, or distant cousins! It's OK! That love-of-you is an energy that will change your frequency, allowing you to feel good about you, never mind them. Now you're no longer denying those old feelings, and you've opened up another space for new thought to enter in.

YESTERDAY'S NEWS

If what we're trying to do here is change our lives, it behooves us to keep asking ourselves why our past seems to be our excuse for not living today. There just isn't any excuse except our comfortable, intellectual addiction to old habits.

The ego, remember, is doing everything in its power to keep the jailhouse wall around us. Go inside and ask why it's so enormously important for you to hang on to all that stuffed pain, and then ask for help in owning it, knowing that the moment you do, the energy is drawn to you to help it happen.

We are, after all, Gods incarnate. But look around in a crowd of people and you'd be hard-pressed to believe that. Scowls, misery, slumps, sulks, and glares—everybody living from their past, operating from habits of pain and fear. That's all it is we hold on to—habits! Any way you look at it, the past is an illusion with no more hold over us than yesterday's news unless we want that hold. You think we don't communicate with ghosts? If we're clutching to the illusions of past events long gone, you better believe we do.

Consider for a moment, with all you've been through to get where you've gotten so far, that just maybe you've learned all there is to learn from your past? Aren't you sort of tired of all that baggage? Then why not get rid of it!

Love it all, bless it all. Go out in the woods, if you can, or into your shower and ask out loud for help in loving that past of yours. "From the Light of God that I am, I call forth help in loving and allowing my past, that I may own it, and release it. So be it." Whether it was what people did to you, or what you did to people, take control of that pain. Go after it, right now. Remember, your point of power is in the present, so opt for life in the Now by welcoming all your past into your present, for release with love.

It takes the same energy to look forward as it does to look backward, but the results are much more splendid. The choice is not up to the ghosts of your past. That's "for victims only." The choice is up to you. If you need help with making the decision to release, you know what to do!

"From the Light of God that I am, I call forth . . ."

CHAPTER 10
SCHOOLHOUSE EARTH

To say that life is filled with challenges seems an absurd understatement. Judging from what most of us have been through, it might be more accurate to say that life is filled with some good-sized obstructions. Yet if we perceive all things, including us, as moving back to God remembered, those obstructions take on a different meaning, for we can then see them as being there for only one reason: to instruct.

Into each lifetime we've brought specific lessons to be learned, along with the expectation of expanding into that greater realization of our God-selves. Both were meant to work hand in hand, lessons leading to expansion. But somebody forgot to tell us that the point is to learn from the lessons and get off the merry-go-round.

One of my best friends on the Program is a grand example of getting off that merry-go-round. Brian came from a wealthy family. From all outward appearances, it would seem he brought to this lifetime the need to learn the major lesson of humility. Growing up in such affluence was not going to make that lesson easy, plus he had an insatiable desire to be a highly prominent and prosperous businessman. These were tough circumstances he'd set for himself, not to mention the disease of alcoholism.

Brian arrested his disease through the Program, but his know-it-all approach to life began to trip him up in his first business, which was on shaky ground. The more he struggled to be a one-man show, the worse his business became until he finally lost it.

He went through it all over again, losing the next business and the next until one day, for reasons he said he could never understand, he began working weekends with the drunks at the downtown mission. Something in him responded to the humbling experience, and he started to let go of ego-control, replacing it with a "let go let God" attitude.

Brian's life, both business and personal, turned around. His Inner Being had pressed him unceasingly until he had thoroughly learned one of his major lessons . . . humility. Undoubtedly, his soul heaved a mighty sigh of relief at not having to put him through it all over again and is now taking him on to greater teachings. It took some heavy banging over the head, but he finally got the message.

Like Brian, I doubt there are many of us who haven't said, "My God, this is happening to me again! I don't get it. What on Earth do I have to do to get out of this rut?" Same relationship problems over and over, same job problems, same money problems, same health problems. And, like the little rubber ball we used to swat as kids, the one attached to its wooden paddle with a rubber string, we've rarely taken time out between bouts.

REMOVING THE REPEAT BAR

Sitting in our energy field is every one of the lessons we brought with us to be learned for this lifetime. They just sit there, hitting the repeat bar over and over until we get it. New script, new players, but same old lessons.

"What did I ever do to deserve this?" "Why me?" "When am I ever going to learn?" Of course, that kind of thinking only reinforces the belief that we're stuck, so that's where we stay. However, it stands to reason that if we've created our problems, we can uncreate them, for they're nothing more than *unrealized experiences.*

That book of life we've carried around with us lifetime after lifetime—known as our soul—has a very clear picture of just what emotions have yet to be experienced to move us back to our Godhood. So it places those requests in the form of frequencies into our energy field, keeping them there until the necessary emotions from the repeated situations are darn-well experienced, understood, and owned.

In the meantime, we magnetize circumstance after similar circumstance to us until at times it seems we're little more than punching bags of unrealized experiences, those lessons yet to be learned. Now, it seems only logical that if we want to stop being the punching bag, we might consider learning the lessons!

For some reason, we haven't gleaned the wisdom from those ever-similar experiences we continue to draw to us. So the particular lesson sits in our energy field, saying, "Hey, in there, anybody home? How many more times are we going to go through this before you get the message? Please! Figure me out so I can leave you alone."

Finally you agree that enough's enough and decide to go to work on it. "In the continual repeat of this thing I seem to go through over and over, what's the lesson I came here to learn? I want answers and I want them now!" You go for walks, you write, you call Home for answers, knowing you have them right there in your soul.

"From the Light of God that I am, I call forth the lesson behind this experience, and I call it forth *now*! So be it."

Then one day, as you're driving home from work giving casual thought to this repetitious problem in your life, perhaps the word "trust" pops into your head. "Trust? What on Earth does that mean, 'trust'? Trust what? Trust who? I trust people, so what does . . . ?"

Maybe it's not perfectly clear at first, but you've learned to listen to that inner voice, so you pay attention, allowing it to unfold. Do you trust yourself? Which self, your ego-self or your God within? Do you trust your Inner Being to handle the details?

To your surprise, your answers are "ego-self" and "no," so you realize you've probably just found a major lesson in back of this repetitious problem. "Trust of my God-self, is it? Well, okay, now let's see . . ."

You decide to try out this business of trust in all your affairs, a little here, a little there. As you get bolder, you begin to insist that your ego-self get out of your way so your God-self can take control. "Let go and let the God you are" becomes the motto of your day.

Soon you realize what was once a major problem is no longer causing those same feelings of fear or aggravation in you any more. You're trusting your God-self to show you the direction. You relax in that trust. The circumstances involved may not have changed yet, but your attitude certainly has, and the change in circumstances will soon follow.

That unrealized experience that's sitting there in your energy field to teach you trust, and bring you experience after experience to learn that trust, starts to diminish in size. Before long, it's gone. It gives you up. The emotion of the lesson, along with the understanding, has been learned. It's recorded in your "book," and your God within heaves a great sigh of relief with a grateful, "Oh, *finally!*"

No matter what the obstruction may be in your life at this moment, whether it's similar to one you've had before or brand-new in nature, simply say to yourself, "All right. I'm faced with something I don't like. Now what's the lesson I'm to learn here? What's it trying to teach me?"

That soul of ours is pressing experiences to us to bring us back to the remembrance of our powers of Mastery, our powers of Godhood. That's why we have experiences, to learn from them *and go on*. Once the wisdom is fully and completely gleaned, the need to repeat the experience is gone forever.

There may be time, however, when old habit patterns left over from a lesson you've already uncovered spring back to life. When you find this happening, put a halt to it any way you can.

I vividly remember one day, while walking down the main street of my California hometown, being suddenly struck for apparently no reason with an old lesson-fear I had already dealt with. At first it frightened me, then it infuriated me. Without thinking, I cried out loud, "Oh no, you don't, you lousy son of a bitch. I know what you are, and I've already owned you, so blast off!" To my great embarrassment, two dear strangers immediately ran over to protect me from my "assailants." It may have been somewhat dramatic, but that particular fear has never returned.

Whenever an already-learned lesson like that pops up to repeat itself, do whatever you have to do to stop it. Call Home for help, go for a walk, talk to the universe, scream at your ego-self, or pray however you pray. If you know with every fiber of your being that once you have gained the wisdom of a lesson, you absolutely do not have to repeat it, you won't. Insist to your ego-self that you no longer need the experience, then feel that release, and know it is finished.

If circumstances still continue to mercilessly repeat themselves, it's only because we have not fully learned all they have to offer, or perhaps we even misidentified the lesson. Spouses keep having affairs, we keep getting fired from jobs, we continue to lose money, we keep banging up our cars.

But whatever the circumstances are, they're not happening again by fate or bad luck; we've magnetized them back into our lives to teach us something. But what? That's our cue to take our focus off the events in order to search more deeply for the lessons behind them. Is it still compassion we need to learn, or self-love, humility, trust, assertiveness? Or is there something more? We go within and ask, knowing the answer lies always in the circumstance, and knowing that the very act of asking will bring the answer, if we watch and listen.

Lessons wear many faces, and we usually have more than one in this lifetime to learn. That's no reason for discouragement, for once you understand the process of seeking the purpose behind each experience in your life, no matter how small or large, you'll know how to quietly evaluate it, reach for its wisdom, own it, and let it go.

Let this become a game, for seriousness is not a qualification for membership in this program. With practice, you can become skilled at finding your purpose in any given situation, from an accident on the freeway to a stubbed toe. Everyday life becomes a whale of a lot more fun because you're in control, accepting the lessons as the teaching games they are, and playing them out to be released into wisdom.

Oh Yes, There *Is* a Purpose

Finally, it sinks in. We're not here on some hit-or-miss roll of the cosmic dice to breathe the heady air of a fresh mountain morn, nor are we here through some stroke of ghastly misfortune to live out life's long, hard road of pre-addiction/post-Program pain. Rather, we're here to learn, and to remember. But lifetime after lifetime our evolutionary process has been painfully slow. Rarely did any of us fully glean the required wisdom of any one life, or we wouldn't be here now. That is our purpose.

Lessons, in the form of experiences or circumstances, began coming to us in early life, but so rapidly did we get caught up in the social-consciousness behavior of building images, we completely shut out what the experiences were wanting to teach us. So, rather than put the lessons behind us early on, we've spent a lifetime creating and protecting these image-shells of what we think we are, such as rich, handsome, abused, smart, successful, fat. These are all limited thoughts which have kept us securely focused as victims of our past and victims of circumstances.

We come here for one reason only, to expand our conscious minds beyond the apparent limitations of life, back into the remembrance that underneath all the masquerading and identities we call reality, we are magnificent, unlimited beings incarnated for the purpose of realizing our Godhood in human form. Once those lights go on, we begin to live life by developing the thoughts that will bring about the realities we want, rather than what our manufactured identities have always dictated. *That* is living our purpose.

Your trusty old soul has your blueprint for this life tucked very securely inside its frequencies, so trust its direction and your Inner Being's guidance. However far afield life seems to take you into its adventures, know from the depths of what you are that "this trip is necessary" to earn the wisdom of the experience. Then you are Master of your life's lessons, and your purpose, the unfolding of your Godhood remembered, is in full swing.

Nothing, but nothing, comes to us that is not meant to be. Lonely? What's the lesson your soul wants you to hear? Need a lover? What's the lesson? Bored? What's your soul trying to tell you? Allow the lessons as they come, and find out what's behind them. They're the "wake-up call" we've all been missing.

HOMEWORK I: STRETCHING

There are some fun things we can do to increase our conscious contact, little tricks of the trade to help us get our old, habitual thinking turned around, back to our God-selves. Some, like "Homework II," can be used daily; others, like this one, as often as possible. I've found both of these exercises to be the most helpful in pulling me back to that place of *Oneness* with my God within where I can then more easily release that tired old stinkin' thinkin'.

Find a secret spot that will be yours and yours alone. Perhaps it's in a woods, or your garden, or on a windy hill. No matter where, find it and make it your very own. Now, when you're set and settled in a comfortable place, without dog, book, or radio, your homework is to just sit . . . and be. That's all, just *be*!

Stay focused in the moment with your thoughts on a flower, or a rock, on anything but your problems or lessons. Then, keeping your mind as blank as you can, reach down inside to your core and feel your roots to God. Feel at one with the universe. Feel the immensity of love around you, even if you have to pretend. Feel a presence, a togetherness.

Start with five to fifteen minutes at first, then longer, as you feel able. With your thoughts focused on your Inner Being, the God you are, push your consciousness out into forever and deliberately feel your enormous Light joining with the Light of the Source. Ride it out hand in hand with your Inner Being. Stretch your thoughts of oneness, become your thoughts, feel your thoughts, be your Life.

We're all Gods incarnate struggling to remember who and what we are. We can struggle blindly with our problems until we opt for bodily death, or we can spend a few minutes alone each day to fill our consciousness with the reality that we are not alone, that we do indeed have a greater purpose in life.

The energy surrounding your body will change by doing this simple exercise, and you will change, for you are radiating a divine power to flood through you like a river, washing away in its higher frequencies all limiting thoughts of every size and description. Purposefully and deliberately you are expanding your conscious contact with your God-self, engaging higher thought, changing your frequency, your life, and you, a little more each time.

HOMEWORK II: THINK GOD

You pick up the mail and there's a bill in there you don't want to open. Little waves of fear grip you in the pit of your stomach. You know it's got to be paid soon, but you're not sure where you'll get the money. Pow! You're back in the habit of fear; the addiction is still there. Whenever that happens, think God.

If someone says something to you that offends you, or you're about to lose your job, or the IRS has called for an audit, or your lover has just announced good-bye, stop in that moment, and think God.

Stepping out of old thinking habits takes a conscious willingness, a focused intent. What you want in those circumstances is new thought, and if you'll just flip your switch to the God channel, it will come, right then and there. Just the act of focusing your mind on your Higher Power within will instantly shift the frequency, opening you to the answers you seek.

Remember, you're a being of free will. An audit from the IRS does not automatically require the comfortable, old habit of fear. Think God, and you implement a basic transfer of energy from the lowest frequency of fear to the higher frequencies of God awareness. All you have to do is do it.

You're creating a force field around you which will either pull in ways to solve your audit or face it without fear. In the midst of chaos, you're reaching down for your reality and changing your frequency. You have new emotions to match your new thoughts, and fear leaves. In other words, by creating new thoughts, the more quieting emotions follow. You're back in control.

Each time we opt for God awareness, rather than ego awareness, we unleash a dynamo of power that builds upon itself, one experience upon another, one call for help upon another, until one day it happens: fear is gone! Now the lesson gives you up for sure, because you've faced it, felt it, and owned it. You've made it happen in consciousness.

It takes only a split second to think God. In that moment, you're aligning with your own power. With practice you'll be able to actually feel a vortex of new energy surrounding and entering your body. No more panic over the IRS, just a "knowing" that you magnetized this to you for some reason, for some lesson to be learned. You find out what that lesson is, own it, and move on.

So think God in any moment throughout the day, and watch the energy of that one empowering thought work wonders.

PRACTICE DOES MAKE PERFECT

In the final analysis, it all boils down to one simple fact: we want to change our lives; we need only to look at, and change, our thoughts and feelings. (Feelings, remember, are the propellants of thought.)

Schoolhouse Earth. We go to any school to learn how to think, so what are you thinking? Job? What are you thinking? Family? What are you thinking? Lover? What are you thinking and feeling?

Granted, we're not going to make a sour relationship better by covering it over with sweet thoughts and feelings. That's denial. But we can call forth, and face, some honest thoughts about the relationship, about us, and most important, about the lessons involved. Then, "From the Light of God that I am, I call forth my direction." What are you thinking? What are you feeling?

There are very few moments in my life now when I don't look at every aspect of what's going on about me as the schoolroom it is: my life as a whole, my day, my circumstances, the people I meet, new friends coming, old friends leaving, world events, what's flowing or working well, what's not flowing or not working well, my health, my attitude, my food, my relationships. How did I create them, or do I view them? How can I change them? What were my thoughts before? What am I thinking and feeling now? Oh yes, there are times when the very last thing I want to admit is that I created a situation by thoughts and feelings alone, but I have only to check back over the days or months, and the cause of whatever's going on is usually annoyingly (or pleasantly) apparent. Then the choice is mine as to how to correct my thought. It's simply a matter of practice.

It goes without saying, the more we put into this course, the faster we're going to learn. To the degree we practice our thinking/

feeling, practice creating, practice conscious contact, practice asking, practice stretching, and practice taking control, will we obtain the full benefits this school has to offer.

"Teach me. Teach me how to change my thinking. Teach me how to change my reality. Teach me how to unleash my honesty. I came here to learn. Help me to learn the power I am. From the Light of God that I am, I call forth my desire to learn. Inner Being, teach me. So be it!"

With practice, we can even take control of our excuses. For instance, how often do you find yourself saying "I can't" instead of "Show me how"? How often do you say "I don't know" instead of "When I find out, I'll let you know"?

Living in excuses does not equate to Masterhood, whether it's never finding a good parking place, or so-called lack of will in dieting. Want to know how powerful you are? Just take a look at what you've created in your life! Now, if you don't like it, find the excuse behind it.

"I can" instead of "I can't." "I will" instead of "Gosh, I don't know how." One of my dearest friends, when faced with either the smallest of challenges in her day or a major life-threatening circumstance, impacts her every move with "Who's the God in this body, anyhow? All right, God I am, watch *this!*" Excuses to this grand God no longer exist. She is absolute Master of her world and life, but it took copious practice in mastering her thoughts for her to get there.

Stop, look, and listen to every thought. The voice of your God within is urging, directing, and prodding, lesson by lesson. It speaks to you in feelings, emotions, wants, desires. When you decide finally to listen, you move into the space of oneness where lessons aren't frightening, where security replaces fear. To go for your masters in

Schoolhouse Earth means to know you have the ability to become whatever you want to become, for if you don't know it, you'll never think it, and if you don't think it, you'll never create the emotions to become it. So, what are you thinking? *"Watch this!"*

"From the Light of God that I am, I call forth understanding of this lesson. So be it!"

"From the Light of God that I am, I call forth the answers which already exist. So be it!"

"From the Light of God that I am, I call forth the means to create a new reality in my life. So be it!"

"From the Light of God that I am, I call forth my joy in each Now. So be it!"

"From the Light of God that I am, I call forth my love of self. So be it!"

"From the Light of God that I am, I call forth my willingness to let this all happen. So be it!"

PERCEPTION, PERCEPTION, PERCEPTION

Whether it's a rude driver on the freeway, or the death of a loved one, all experiences—every single one—are there to move us away from focusing on, and reacting to, *out-there* circumstances. Sooner or later we come to fully accept that the action is always *in here*, not *out there*. Out there is only our perception.

We perceive circumstances as bad or good, depending on the effects they have on us. "I was terrified when I got that letter" means we perceived a bad event coming which would cause us to feel deep concern. On the other hand, "I was so proud watching the kids graduate" denotes a good situation, for that's how we felt—good.

So we label an event in direct relation to how we perceive it to be. Then we label our reaction within the circumstance as right or wrong. "I handled that one well, but really blew it over there." All day long we unconsciously and mercilessly judge the nature of our reality, and ourselves, by good or bad, right or wrong. It's a habit guaranteed to keep us stuck.

When we view something as wrong, or bad, we automatically judge it to be negative. Now, if we're the one who created the event, we rush to wrap ourselves in a massive robe of guilt, and a whole new spiral of events is created from how we perceived the event to be. The trust is, it's impossible for us to do anything wrong, or even right, for that matter. It's only our perception that made it so. What we do simply *is*, for the experience of the lesson.

Take mistakes, for instance. Or wrong decisions. There's no such thing! Rights and wrongs are what pull us into an event, getting us emotionally involved in all the gooey drama, rather than just allowing the event to be, seeing the purposeful good in it, and learning to change our perception of it. In other words, what we perceive, we believe; what we believe, we are. But there are no rights or wrongs; there simply *is!*

With this attitude, we can take ourselves out of the judgment of everything that happens to, or around us, and quietly move back into our own center to watch whatever it is unfold. After all, that's what dramas are for, to get us to stop seeing them as right or wrong, good or bad, but simply allow that they are. The events of the drama are meaningless except for the practice in perception. There is no good or bad. Those are judgments based in limited thinking coming straight from the delighted ego, causing us to react according to our judgments.

In fact, your God-self never reacts. It allows, because it doesn't see right or wrong, it simply *is*. It doesn't see levels of good-better-best. To your God, there is only the "isness" life. It is Friend Ego that does all the reacting and judging, so when you're viewing an event with any kind of judgment, know your ego is cutting loose and having a heyday. If you're wanting to find peace in life and expand your God within, step back, take yourself out of the event, and allow.

You have never failed, nor are you going to fail. Not one among us has ever failed at anything. There's no such thing. And mistakes? No such thing. Only experiences that shout, "What did you learn? Did you get past the image, the ego, to a mode of detached observation, or did you merge into the juicy drama and become the character?"

The universal law of consciousness and energy says that what we focus on expands. So focus on your perception of the negative in an event, and guess what you'll get!? Focus on what the event is trying to tell you, and your God-self will make it very clear. No grades, no rights or wrongs, no goods or bads, no mistakes or failures, just lessons we continue to magnetically draw to us until we learn.

WINNING YOUR MASTERS

Up to now, we've been students, bumping into obstacles, staying out of dramas, listening to our thoughts, calling for answers. The next step is to become the teacher.

Right now, as we take a close look at our lives, and challenges, and lessons, not to mention the retraining of our thoughts, it all seems quite enough to handle, if not overwhelming. Yet a strange thing happens as we start this new way of life. Desire grows!

Though it may seem impossible to conceive that you would ever want more to handle than you have right in this moment, the day is not far off when you'll want to go even further, sometimes as fast as you can get there. It's a divine phenomenon of passion, of will, of the awakening God-self saying, "Well, heck, this isn't so bad. What's next? Bring it on . . . *now!*"

When you start seeing the events in your life as nothing more than the games of your self-directed dramas, you get curious, and something in you (guess what) says, "Hey, wouldn't it be fun to experiment with that power?!"

You start thinking about all the unfinished business in your life, the unfinished lessons, the things you have yet to learn that you've not even thought of, and suddenly you want it all. You want completion. You want it finished. And you want it *now!*

When that day comes, when you sit in the wind and tell it you know you've never gone in a wrong direction any more than it has, that you've never been good or bad any more than it has, and that you've never failed any more than it has, then you're ready to speak from the Light of God that you are, as total Master.

Now comes the biggest test of all, and you make the decision, by God, to go for it. You ask the God of your being to bring forth all that you have yet to face in this schoolhouse of Earth.

And why not? There's no fear now, only the burning passion to awaken that sleeping God within. There are no obstructions, only lessons. So you plug in, take a deep breath, and call it forth:

> *From the Light of God that I am,*
> *I call forth, in gentleness and peace,*
> *all that has yet to be cleared in my life*
> *to bring me to the remembrance*
> *of that which I am. So be it!*

It is a moment to remember. When it comes, as it does to all of us who pursue this course with hunger, you have graduated from this term with honors. You are in total control of your school, your lessons, your growth, your pace, and . . . your life!

Congratulations. You have just earned your master's degree from Schoolhouse Earth.

CHAPTER 11
THE POWER OF EMOTION

When I first began this journey, one of my teachers said to me, "Beloved woman, know that the truest treasure of this life is emotion." Now, I had always prided myself on being contained and felt his comment was grossly out of line. Why would you allow yourself to be out of control, emotionally drooling all over the place, when you could be stoic as I was and take life on the chin?

As time went on and strange new feelings began to stir inside me, I became frightened. Something was knocking at my inner door, and I had no desire to find out who or what it was. Or why! My surface anger and other outward displays of feelings notwithstanding, true emotional release was a perfect stranger to me, and to open the door to its entry into my life presented an unknown of fearful proportions.

Eventually, of course, I turned that around and saw clearly what he meant by "truest treasure." It became obvious that as addictive personalities, we continue to wear those blinders against our inner selves, even after years on the Program. The fear of releasing a torrent of unknown monsters upon our sensitive selves is more than most of us care to think about. It's old pain, unknown pain, forgotten pain, and future shock, all wrapped up into one ugly, cancerous tumor we hold tightly within us, often straight to our graves.

Therein I found the secret to my addiction, that sure enough, emotion is what life's all about. Stuff it, as we are wont to do, and it will ooze its life-draining poisons to keep us among the living dead. Allow it, feel it, or even become it, and we fling open the floodgates to release the magnificence of everything that we are.

THE CURSE OF DENIAL

No doubt about it, "denial" has become a highly prized buzzword in recovery circles and talk shows. Go to an Al-Anon meeting, and what are they talking about? Denial. Go to an ACOA meeting, and what are they talking about? Denial. It's the "in" problem we've all practiced (and are just now finding out to what enormous extent!). But what is it that happens to our being, our God, our soul, or even our ego, when we deny?

Once again we start from the premise that what we are is not the body we inhabit, but what we feel! And yet, can you remember the last time during your growing up years when your parents or any close adult said to you, "Honey, what is that you're feeling? Think about it now, and go ahead and feel it and express it, because it will make you feel better." Not a chance! We were told to keep that stiff upper lip, or worse, given the obligatory pat on the head, or the piece of apple pie, guaranteed to make us feel better. So we compensated. We just turned the tables. If *feeling* wasn't OK, we soon found that reacting was.

We reacted internally and externally to everything in our family environment from the premise that feelings were downright dangerous. From then on, the pattern was set. Don't feel, just react. What a way to live! We shut down and operated from only a minute portion of our enormous emotional repertoire. For the rest of our lives we could react from only a few tried-and-true cards in our emotional deck, leaving the rest of the stack untouched. To this day, no matter what the situation is, we continue to use only those same few but trusted emotions, therefore magnetizing circumstances to us from only those same limited frequencies. And we wonder why life seems so dull and repetitious. Same old emotions; nothing new allowed.

Even once we get to the Program, we barely scratch the surface of our emotional hotbeds, thinking the time we have, and the inventories we've taken, will make it all better. Obviously, if we don't know something more is in there, we can't pull it up. What's the secret, then, to uncovering what's been so securely hidden? What's the secret to opening the doors—without fear—to the indescribable joy of allowing, embracing, and living life on full emotional throttle?

There are many forms of denial. There's denial of one's current feelings, denial of past feelings, denial of a current truth, denial of a desire, denial of a dislike, and so on. Let's start with current feelings, for in understanding how we constantly deny even those, it will be easier for us to dig down to what's been so long repressed—and consequently stuck—in our energy fields.

Your boss lays you off for lack of work in the shop. You know what he says is the truth, but you have a hard time not taking it as a personal affront. You're angry, hurt, and scared, but decide not to let it out since it was, after all, only a layoff, not a firing. You go home, tell your spouse and yourself, "It's OK, I'm OK, I'm really calm about the whole thing."

It won't work. You can't be filled with rage and fear, then try to say you're filled with peace, and expect results. You've got to experience the feeling, no matter what it is, or how rotten it might make you feel. In every case. Every time. You have to *feel the feelings* or you're just on ice, with no way to make contact with your Inner Being.

Or maybe you had a fine day at work, but on your way home you feel angry and don't know why. Do something as soon as you can to express, and experience the feeling. Allow it to be, embrace it, work it through. If you do this honestly, and call for help in the process, the reasons for your anger will come to you (like a sense of powerlessness over some situation, as is so often the case with anger), and you can own and release it into wisdom. Feel the feelings! Think about them, then feel them.

It doesn't mean you have to act on them. Call for help. What are the feelings telling you? How are they identified with your image? How much of a habit are they? Where do you experience them in your body? Get into them, but never, never stuff them.

So much for the layoff and coming-home angers which were known feelings. Now, what about the unknown ones that pop in and out that we don't want to feel or face and have turned our backs on for so long? Remember, in back of every feeling is a vibrating thought or belief, known or unknown. So now what?

PROCESSING YOUR FEELINGS

To process a feeling, the first step is to trust it, because it's trying to tell you something. What can it do to you? Scare you a little, perhaps. Be painful? Possibly. But punch out your lights? Never. Indeed, it's time to stop running from these stuffed shadows of our past. We'll face them and process them. Processing a feeling has three basic steps:

1) *First comes trust, of yourself, of your feelings, of your God within that's saying, "It's going to be OK for you to feel these things. It's OK! No matter what or how strong they are, you'll survive and recover."*

2) *Next, allow the thought or feeling and don't judge it, no matter how horrid it may be. Allow it. It's neither right nor wrong, good nor bad; it just is.*

3) *And finally, accept ownership of the feeling and all it has to offer, without fear, without panic, in love, in anticipation. You created it, so accept it as a part of you. You don't have to act on it, just allow the feeling to be there and notice nothing awful happens as a result. Feelings are not facts; they are simply our own creations asking for attention and love.*

You may want to place yourself inside a ring of Light for safety and comfort as you begin to process feelings. That embraces you securely in the electromagnetic field of your Inner Being. Then, from that place of security, let the feeling come forth for exploration and understanding. If you experience fear at delving into an unknown emotion, allow the fear to be. You have your Inner Being as well as all heaven with you, so get into it, own it, and make it yours in wisdom, lest in hiding it owns you forever.

Practice is the big word. Be aware of denying emotion in the midst of any event, and make the decision of a Master to stop doing it. We're so accustomed to participating in the event, we tactfully ignore the powerful electromagnetic thoughts being stuffed. With practice, however, we can allow ourselves to feel the full emotion of any thing, or any event, past or present, and stop going unconscious. Remember, denial comes straight from our ego-selves, so the safety we want to have in releasing that emotion comes by calling for inner strength in the very moment of whatever's happening around us.

We need to get hold of denial on a grand scale and to be completely committed to ending it in every aspect of our lives. Pretending we don't really feel what we've stuffed is like trying to keep smoldering sticks of dynamite inside a bottle in hope of stopping the explosion. Until those emotions are recognized, experienced, felt, owned, and released, all we do is call them to us again and again. We deny it; we get it back.

Denial is happening when anything is going on in your world that you don't want to accept. You're having a "lesson," and you ignore it. Denial. You want to say something to someone, but the image says, "Oh no, what would they think?" Denial. You decide that everything in a situation is "fine," when your reality is hollering at you with emotions of a different color. Denial. You're mad at someone and don't express it. Denial. You really want to stay home, but don't express it. Denial. You feel you must accept something whether you like it or not. Denial. And with denial, goes victim, victim, victim, completely owned and enslaved by what's being denied.

Our God-self is working overtime to draw our newly expressed desires to us, but those denied emotions are so strong in our energy fields they override, and severely block, our powers to manifest. Everything's on hold. Separation is still in high gear, for the ego is reigning supreme, quite content with its high-handed control. All this because of our fear to feel old feelings, or express new ones as we truly want to do.

Denial is lack of self-love in the extreme. When we deny any of our feelings, past or present, we don't allow the release of what was taken in long ago, or even yesterday. Yet when denial is faced and put to an end, the ego finally takes a back seat to the power of the God-self, and the new power, with its infinitely higher vibrations, can finally get through the energy field.

RELEASING DENIAL

The fear of facing stuffed emotions is always greater than the actuality of feeling them. The beauty is they don't have to be acted out, just acknowledged and felt. That in itself is a form of release, allowing your consciousness to expand. Now there's movement in your energy field; nothing is stagnant. But perhaps the greatest benefit is the enormous feeling of accomplishment and self-empowerment that one experiences when those first steps of expression are taken.

The trick is to work both ends against the middle in this business of releasing, emotions from the past and emotions of the now (which include feelings projected towards the future, such as worry). Watch them like a hawk in everything you do. Each time you have a decision to make, no matter how small, check out the feelings with your Inner Being, rather than operating out of emotional habit from your rational ego-mind. Do this two hundred times a day, if need be, until you get the idea that inner feelings are straight from your God-self. They're your intuition, power centers or "thought-balls" of divine energy, you need never fear. Go within, ask, listen, and know you're safe. When you get in the habit of trusting your inner self, you do what you feel, or sense, to be true. There's no better way to put an end to denial of feelings than by practicing the reality of their existence!

Feelings talk to you and give you understanding. By learning to listen to them, you're bridging the gap between your ego-self and God-self. Deny feelings, and you short-circuit that bridge. As often as you can, wherever you are and whatever you're doing, go within and listen. Then allow yourself the rare joy—yes, joy—of feeling your rage, or anger, or jealousy, or whatever other so-called negative emotion may hit you in the face from past or present. Only in the feeling of it, and then expression if it's appropriate, can you release it. Only in the owning of it, will it give you up.

When that time comes when you would normally remain silent, or ignore a feeling, say to your Inner Being, "Now! I need help right now." With this call you're jumping in to open up all the channels to start that stagnant energy moving. If your release is through verbal expression, don't stop until you're completely finished. The act of feeling or expressing is not going to hurt you, but it may kill you if you don't. So acknowledge, call for help, feel, and express.

Now, here's the bonus: every time you take a step into the unknown by expressing evenly and honestly, you turn up the frequency knob of self-love. Everything in you vibrates a little faster until one day you find yourself expressing something—with love, even in anger—that in your wildest dreams you could never have imagined before. What a monkey off your back! What a glorious feeling!

A little trick I've used, with great success, to dissolve blocks, fears, or denials is to give them a formal ceremonial release by speaking them out loud. This creates an assertive declaration to your subconscious that you mean business, and it responds immediately. Call forth your Inner Being for the ceremony to give the release greater power. Then, speaking out loud, declare that you no longer believe in the old feelings, you no longer want them, and you lovingly release them forever. " . . . and so, from the Light of God that I am, I willingly release you, and set you free forever. So be it."

UNFINISHED BUSINESS

There's another kind of insidious denial, the denial of self. In one way, it's a physical denial, but in another, it too is denial of feelings, for we live in the feelings of our lacks, lack of money, love, prestige, desired career, whatever. We stay there, denying ourselves what we really want out of life, because we rarely hold still long enough to find out what that is.

This is major soul business we're talking about, not just wishful thinking. If there's something you've always wanted to do, that's your soul telling you it's an experience you need, a piece of growth that's unfinished. Do it! To deny yourself that special experience is denial of your soul's intent, the greatest form of personal deprivation. You want to take a Kon Tiki around the world? Do it! You want to climb Mount Everest? Find a way to do it! You want to own a pie shop? Do it. These are vitally important desires (emotions) wanting to be realized, adventures waiting to be lived for the particular emotional experience that awaits and the lessons to be learned.

These deep, often secret, desires may represent a hidden talent that's never been expressed or a particular emotion never realized, perhaps over many lifetimes. Your soul will keep pressing you into action, through desire, to open yourself to those desires, for they may represent a major expansion in your evolutionary process, or the desires may simply represent a page that needs to be lived for a particular experience to be learned.

Finding ways to live these desires will make your life richer, sweeter, and a whole lot more fun. They're not just your crazy ideas or wild daydreams. They're your God within calling you to wrap up some unfinished business, to finish with something you need to do. Play in the band, stain the glass, write the book, hike the trail. To keep saying, "I've always wanted to . . . ," is a straight line to sickness in body and spirit, for your whole being is once again being denied. So instead of always wanting to . . . , consider calling forth the ways and means to manifest the experience, even if it means changing your whole existence to do it.

Whatever those denied emotions or desires—known or unknown—may be, find them, face them, feel them, own them, perhaps live them, and release them. If the release is complete, your energy will change dramatically, and everything in your world and daily routine will take a surge forward in breathtaking freedom.

So let all the emotions come. Allow yourself to experience the wisdom that comes from the emotion of anything, for in the emotion lies our "truest treasure of life." We are not what we inhabit; we are what we feel! Emotion—realized thought—unhampered and pure in its flow, is the path to God remembered. No one walks that path but you.

ENERGY MOVEMENT: DOORWAY TO FREEDOM

In thinking about releasing past or present emotions, it behooves us to remember the stuff of which we're made, consciousness and energy. Energy, of course, is the activity of God-power, and consciousness is what moves it. Our goal, then, is to learn how to manipulate our energy and move into a new realm of existence, the realm in which we were meant to live, yet the very one we've forgotten.

Thinking of ourselves as nothing but energy is not easy. It goes against everything we've ever known or believed about our reality, yet even scientists now accept that the human body is a force field of tremendous cosmic power. What they don't yet accept is that our energy can be consciously manipulated to change our entire physical and emotional being.

Indeed, we can move our own energy any time and any place we desire. We can move it about and outside our body, through and inside our body, or both. We can move it slowly, rapidly, or hold it still. We can move it out to infinity to fill the cosmos or pull it into a specific point in, or outside, our body. The object is to move it as often and in as many creative ways as we can imagine. This is done simply by "seeing" it in our mind's eye. By visualizing that movement, we are literally making it happen!

To begin the process of energy moving, it helps to see that energy as light . . . brilliant, phosphorescent, pure, white light. That way you're not just trying to move empty space and have something more visually tangible to hang onto in your imagery. Try it now, if you like, and play with it. You can use the exercise that follows.

Light Visualization

For instance, see yourself encased in a white ball of light and move it all around you . . . up, down, out in front of you, under you, etc. Now make it flat and whiz it around you like an electric fan, first one direction, then the other. Then spin it around you horizontally, like a top. Now turn it into a rod and loop it up through your spine, out your head, and back around to the base of your spine (a superb exercise for opening the brain, by the way). Now turn it into a figure eight and loop the bottom down into Mother Earth and the top way out into the cosmos, with you in the middle. Now put it in a tiny round ball behind your heart and stretch it up just outside the top of your head, then out beyond infinity. If you want a really trippy experience, put a pyramid of light (any size) on the top of that rod and let it sit about six inches from the top of your head for as long as you can hold the image.

Play, experiment, have fun, and it won't be long before you'll actually feel the movement that your imagery has created, maybe tingles in the head, or hands, or a dizziness, even nausea.

Aside from expanding our imagining skills (one of our most precious God-skills), what's the purpose of doing this? The movement of energy helps to release what's been stuck in our subconscious. We're making waves, stirring everything up, loosening the old, emotional energy patterns for easier removal. In fact, whenever we want to accomplish anything in consciousness, we need only begin to think energy and start moving our light around to set the stage. It's like using warm water to soak a food-caked baking dish. The water softens the old food for removal, just as swishing our energy around softens old patterns for removal.

Energy moving is also one of the easiest and most important ways to begin raising your vibratory frequency, for the more you stir it up, the more unseen Light you draw to you. The more Light you draw into your magnetic field, the greater will be your own magnetic properties (magnetism) that arc to the mind of God. You're bringing yourself into alignment with the powers of the universe while firing up your own powers within. It's the simplicity and magnificence of the life-force spiral.

Thought creates energy. So as we give conscious thought to energy, in other words, contemplate it or focus on it, the energy all about us increases, as does the magnetism of the field which surrounds us. As our magnetism increases, so does our desire. As our desire increases, so does our energy flow, and we're right back to the beginning of the spiral, only this time at a higher level. We have our motor started, it picks up momentum, and finally rhum, rhum, rhum, rhum, wham! we're out of our old frequency, and into a new level where something inside says, "Hey, you want to get rid of that old stuff now? Great! Go for it; the timing's just right."

Before you start running energy, however, there are some things to watch for. Those old ideas have formed into such huge crystallizations of heavy static in your energy field; when you start the process of release, you may feel actual physical pain manifesting almost anywhere in your body. You might acquire a strange twitch or find yourself starting to shake momentarily for no reason. Fevers, heavy colds, and come-and-go headaches (with or without my so-called spikes) are also common. I had such extreme pain in my hands and feet when I first started moving energy that for weeks the piercing pains woke me up at night. The worst of it lasted for a month and was gone altogether in about ten weeks. So don't be concerned. You're simply experiencing a physical reaction to the unaccustomed movement of energy about your body and the literal shaking loose of those old, stuck "thought balls." While your God-self will be saying, "It's about time," your body may not understand for a while.

HAPPY ANGER, HAPPY BODY

It's stagnant emotions that cause unhappy states. So whenever you set about to have a good anger or depression, it's important to keep that energy moving and not hold it back to stagnate again. In other words, if you're going to have it, have it and be done with it.

Anger is one of the greatest motivators known to mankind, provided, of course, it's expressed in a healthy way and not stuffed. So allow it to be felt and expressed, even if you have to find a safe place to do it. The very fact we can feel anything is a gift from God more remarkable than life itself, and as long as you keep it moving, that energy is swishing around nicely into release.

Be sure to watch if you're expressing "dirty" or "clean" anger. Dirty anger is straight blame, where we take no responsibility for our emotions. Clean anger is making the conscious decision that we have a desire to express feelings and to take full responsibility for both the intensity of the emotion and the consequences. One is victim; the other is Master.

But it's the body that can be your greatest ally in anger. You'll find many stuffed emotions wanting to release directly through the body, so let them come in whatever way the body directs. Beat a pillow, make love, go for a walk, cry, or sing for joy. If you listen to your body, it will tell you what it wants to do, when it's had enough, and when it's finished. By allowing the physical responses to flow, you're moving quantities of energy which will avoid a lot of new stuffing.

Then, after you've experienced the physical release, rest for a while and be watchful of any new thoughts that may move across your mental movie screen. If more emotion starts to pop up, let it come, and release it as the body suggests. Remember, the event is long gone; it's the feelings you've created and held onto that have been causing the trouble. So give your body a chance, and let it go to work for you.

Anger isn't wrong, yet most people are so blocked emotionally that the thought of any sort of healthy expression terrifies them (it certainly used to terrify me!). Actually, a conscious decision to choose anger can be exciting and just plain fun. So acknowledge your feelings, express them with the help of your Inner Being, and get them moving. Nothing more need be done with them. Now as you move through those emotions, you'll begin to see how the beauty of life is in motion, not in stagnation.

THE EMOTION OF FEAR

So far, we've only talked around it: Fear, that biggest of all monsters that seems to hold us in eternal bondage and so delights our ego in playing the game of denial.

We harbor only two emotions, love and fear. Under the catch-all umbrella of fear comes the long list of everything that love isn't, such as depression, anxiety, rage, jealousy, etc. What isn't love is fear. There is no other truth. And when we run from any kind of fear, we never get a chance to find out what's chasing us. We just feel the ghastly effects. However, when we finally refuse to run, and agree with our Inner Being that we're going to stay with the emotions until they're fully felt and understood, they begin to dissolve in normal fashion to make room for new energy.

Fear is just a state of mind. That's all it is. It's the most powerful of doors that closes us off from the Light of our Inner Being and the one that requires the most concentrated effort to release. But there is one activity that almost always works in relation to releasing fear, and that is to talk to it, out loud.

Fear is always some kind of lesson. If we want to get rid of it, we have only to find out what the lesson is we're to learn. So we make a decision to take a few minutes off from our fear of the fear and realize that it's trying to teach us something. By doing this, we're allowing this powerful energy to become our teacher, addressing it as something helpful to us, as a force that has the ability to assist us in making quantum leaps over spiritual ground. Now it becomes our best friend. Indeed, fear will always teach us if we'll let it.

Begin by checking out where in your body you're feeling the fear. It's never throughout your entire body, even though you're positive you've been dunked, submersed, washed, and bathed in it. Fear is always localized, like a hurt finger, and it's important you start to think of it just that way. A hurt finger is not you, it's just a hurt finger that's gotten banged up. The rest of you is fine.

Now start talking to it. What makes it smaller, what makes it larger, what started it, who comes to mind when you think about it, what events come to mind, and what will it take to get it calmed down? If you ask it to, it will talk back in the form of dreams, ideas, promptings, or new feelings. Your fear is not you, any more than your hurt finger is you. Fear is an emotion localized in some specific place in your body. By finding out where your fear is, and of what it's comprised, you're acknowledging the emotion so it can move through you.

After you've talked to it, now comes the time to express it, in whatever way your body (through your Inner Being) suggests, but above all, don't hide from it. (At one time, I had "Feel Your Fears" Post-It notes all over the house, car, and workshop to stop my incessant hiding from it.) Run your energies about you and, with the help of your Inner Being, state out loud, " . . . my fear used to be . . . , and I now willingly release it and choose love."

We had some wonderful expressions in my Home Group about fear, though I must admit I never fully understood the depth of their wisdom until now. For instance, "Do the thing you fear, and the death of fear is certain." Or, "Fear is False Evidence Appearing Real . . . F.E.A.R." Or, "Fear went to the door, and Faith answered." They all say the same thing, that it's our fear of fear that keeps us so fearful because it keeps us so separated from our own divine power. Press yourself to feel the fear. That's the only way it can move through you. If you give fear the chance to pass through you, it will. Then just settle down with your Inner Being to find out what that fear's been trying to tell you.

Releasing fear is a matter of reaching down past its grip to the Source within us where no fear exists, only love. That unconditional love lies quietly waiting in the center of our being. Once we've tapped into it soundly and surely, we never fear again.

LOVE: GRANDEST EMOTION OF ALL

Is there one among us who hasn't been searching for love? We hang on to our relationships fearing we'll lose that once wonderful feeling, so we become addicted to the person for whom we had love, thinking if he or she leaves, we'll never have that feeling again. Then the person leaves because we've given him or her the responsibility of generating this feeling in us. So we try another, and another, always relying on someone else to light our fires, always looking outside ourselves to fill that void, for all we've ever been taught is that human love . . . and even God's love . . . comes from *out there*.

Actually, love is not something we *do*, flicking it on and off like a light bulb, one day on, and the next day off. That's ego-emotion. Love is the stuff of which we're made.

While we call love an emotion, in reality it's an energy, and the emotion we experience when we allow ourselves to feel that energy is only the result of tapping into the flow, as one might tap into hot circuitry. Stick your wet finger into a turned-on light socket and you'll get mighty emotional—fast! Same thing with tapping into and igniting the energy of love. It's feeling the flow of what we already are and can't possibly undo because it's our very essence.

In the human body, the energy of love is localized in the area of the heart. In fact, by strongly focusing your consciousness in laser-beam fashion toward any being, you can actually make that heart area heat up and even feel as if you had a mustard plaster on your chest. All you're doing is moving energy—in this case, the energy and high frequency of love—with your consciousness. Now comes the fun. Once you view love as an actual energy, and begin to consciously control its focus, this oft-talked-about but rarely understood art of "loving yourself" takes on a whole new light, for when you start this energy into motion, you automatically start to love yourself!

The energy of love is actually an observable magnetic field (it's been photographed!) that moves through us, around us, radiates out of us, and changes everything when it's activated. *It's the highest vibratory frequency in the omniverse.* Any person, no matter how much he dislikes himself or how depressed he may be, can call for and feel this energy build-up throughout his being as it wells up from within and without. Anyone, at any time, can learn to move it and activate it. Anyone! It's simply moving energy with consciousness, tapping into it at will.

We *are* love. It's not in our sex organs, but alive and quite well within us, shining brightly against even our darkest fears, but held back from expression and feeling by our denials. It's not something we learn, for there has never been a time when we didn't know it! It's always been within us, the core of what we are, every day, every night, through every crisis, in the midst of every fear. We have only to learn to activate it, and in an instant, it will expand to touch everything and everyone in our lives.

When I began this way of life, I'd sit for hours pondering what love was and how to make it come alive in me. I loved being loved by my spiritual teachers, for I couldn't yet feel it toward myself. While I truly believed I was a loving person with a grand love for myself, those surface beliefs never had a chance in the face of my own deep-rooted fears and self-denials.

One day, on my precious hill where I'd go to think about it all, I declared out loud (hoping I'd really hear myself), "I am loved." I sat with that thought for a long time, repeating the words with all the awareness I could muster, when suddenly the most amazing thing happened. In the midst of a cold, piercing wind, my body started to heat up. The heat built gradually, becoming so intense that even my toes got sweaty from the sharp rise in body temperature. I stayed with the thought, held on to it, moved around in it, and forced myself to feel the love that I was telling myself I had. My eyes burned, my head was on fire, and I was drenched. The longer I held on to the feeling, the hotter I got until suddenly there came an indescribable moment when I felt as if I was wrapped in the arms of God itself. Instantly, the heat was gone.

Although I didn't know what was happening at the time, the heating of my body was, of course, my energy field vibrating at faster and faster speeds as I accepted the higher thoughts into my body.

And the sweats came as the unexperienced thought from the unknown was becoming realized in my body. Then the ecstasy, the *climax*, so to speak, came as the thought was fully accepted. I was allowing the God of my Being to come through. That's all, just allowing my own love, the highest vibratory frequency in the omniverse of which I am a part, to take over. And for a precious few moments, it did.

So, while love can't be learned (since we already are "it"), we can indeed practice ways to draw that force from within and about us to change our energy fields to higher vibrations. And perhaps most important, we can practice the decision to love, the decision to generate from our own being what we've been so desperately looking for outside of ourselves.

But before getting into the "how to's" of activating and moving this supreme energy, a lighthearted warning. Most of our lives, we've sought others to fill that void within us by "needing" someone to make us feel complete. The fact is, once we ignite that magnificent central core of our being and start to live in the flow of its divine energy, need drops away, and often so do needy relationships. So take gentle heed; activating this energy may prove hazardous to your relationship!

THE LOVE GAME

There was a time in my own searching when, if I had come across one more book telling me that all I had to do was "love myself more," I would have hired the nearest hit man to obliterate the publishers. Love myself more; poppycock! They tell you that's what you should do but never tell you how. I wanted that love-of-self feeling with a fervor and was ready to go to any lengths to find it.

One of the techniques I uncovered in my search is so simple, yet so powerful, it's truly laughable. While you, too, may find humor in this unique exercise, if you want to tap into and release that magnificent power within as much as I did, give it a try. It will absolutely turn the tide of your lack of self-love and self-worth if you'll play the process out completely. And it will set a new energy about you that you'll find downright remarkable as you encounter the new high frequencies.

Here's how it goes. Get into your feelings the glow you get when you suddenly see an old friend you haven't seen for a long time. Experience that warm joy of giving them a huge, delicious bear hug. Or if you have a favorite uncle or aunt you adore but haven't seen for a year or more, feel what it's like to open the door and see them standing there. Feel how happy and full that moment is as you freely embrace, and the love pours from you to them. If you're OK with that same sort of feeling with either of your parents, put them into the picture, but only if you're OK with them and can express your love openly through the spontaneity of that happy bear hug.

Got the feeling? Good. Now, take a walk to town, to the supermarket, to the office, to anywhere where there are people. Find someone you don't know, but can clearly see coming towards you, and *visualize* yourself running up and giving that person the hug of his or her life, your long-lost friend or relative hug. There's no surprise, for there's a deep connection between you, an old sweet bond of love, as close as old, old friends. Feel that love with everything in you. Feel the joy. Feel the warmth. Hold that person tightly in your imagined embrace as the love pours from your heart and soul.

Even though you've only visualized this, a perfect stranger has just allowed you to actually ignite that energy and start it flowing. Your force field instantly changes to a much higher vibratory frequency, and your problems momentarily take a back seat to the beauty of the Now. Without ever knowing what hit them, your strangers have just received a jolt of your energy, wondering what they just walked through. Often targets will turn around and smile at the person next to them or look up wistfully, as if suddenly hit by the thought of an old friend. Remember, you're not only sending them love, you're experiencing it by visualizing your arms around them in a joyous embrace. That's what is freeing your force field, for you're consciously activating that flow of energy. The movement is clearly outward. You've put your energy-plug straight into the universal socket, and everything's zipping and zapping in response.

You'll probably start, as I did, with "safe" strangers, you know, the kind you wouldn't mind going to lunch with if you had to. Once you get those down pat, move on to some who are less safe, people you think might have B-O or are "beneath" you in life. If this is threatening to you, stay in the safety zone for a while with comfortable targets before moving on. If a different race or sex is normally threatening to you, be sure to include some person that meets these criteria. And don't forget the bag ladies, or the town drunk who hangs out on the corner. Move always to more challenging souls and let the waves of love pour out of you in torrents of unhampered joy.

You'll find that your feelings will grow with practice because your energy field is becoming accustomed to the higher vibrations. Fear in all areas of your life begins to drop away because you're bombarding your field with new vibrations which replace—each time and for a longer time—the old thought forms of fear and doubt.

When you think you have this exercise mastered and can get the energy moving at the drop of a hat, really feeling your love flow in the warm desire to embrace, remember: what you think you are feeling for another, you are feeling for yourself!

You absolutely cannot feel love for another unless you can first feel it for yourself. That's the only way the brain can compute. You feel it inside, but you are identifying it by thought from fantasized outward actions: thought, to brain, to central nervous system, to soul for identification, back to brain, spelled "love." Again, *that love you're feeling for another is what you are feeling for yourself.* You can't love *out there* and not have love *in here.*

It's the same thing when you say, "I can love others, but I can't love myself." You're speaking of a physiological impossibility. You may think you don't love yourself, but if you can feel tenderness for your cat, or compassion for your sick neighbor, the joy of the fantasized street-corner embrace, or even momentary love of a new day, these are mirrors reflecting your own love of yourself. Where we get into trouble and block that flow is in saying, "I don't love myself." That's like a red light going on in the middle of a fast-moving freeway. Screech, bang, crash! The love energy can't get out into consciousness flow because we've turned on the red light.

The secret to activating that energy center is simply to become aware of it and realize it's no big mystery. It is, that's all. It just is. The minute you think about it, you're plugged in. That's why the hug-a-stranger exercise is so important; when you can plug in at will, you're the Master. Now it's love in motion, and everything you do manifests from that state of consciousness, joy, happiness, abundance. It comes because you have chosen for it to come. You've made a conscious decision to love out of choice, not out of need.

The basic quality of our being is love, so what you're practicing here is not how to love but how to activate it. No one is incapable of love, or he wouldn't exist—afraid of love, maybe, but not incapable of it. The minute you find it inside and keep it moving, you become love in action. And if it's moving through you, who can take it from you? The more you release, the more you'll have. Energy creates energy. So you can either participate in love's growth within you or spend time worrying about the lack of it. The choice is always yours.

The power of that energy flow is absolutely magical. It affects every cell in your body. It heals. It transforms. It turns fear aside. It shines Light in the darkest corners of loneliness. It spawns courage for new adventure. It says, "I am." Of course, you don't have to be hugging a stranger to activate the energy flow. Just by concentrating on the area of your body from which the flow emanates (the heart center), you'll activate it. And it goes without saying, the more you do it, the greater the buildup about you.

When you're resting, think pointedly about the heart area, or think about it when you're having some quiet time on a hilltop. Feel the movement of it all, and pretty soon it won't matter if others love you or not, because you're becoming so deeply loving of your own self. Make the energy move out from you to embrace a flower, or a cloud, a dewdrop on a rose, your baby's face, or the overture to *Tannhäuser*; the more you deliberately, consciously, purposefully move that energy out to anything or anybody, the more love you're stoking in that generator inside for even greater flow. And by the way, if you could see that energy in action (as many do), you'd see undulating waves of radiant pink building wave upon wave as you pump it out.

We are energy generators, so why not generate for our own benefit rather than run on automatic for the benefit of everyone else? Consciousness and energy! All we have to do is learn to harness it, and we stop *needing* what we can readily generate within ourselves. There's an enormous relief that comes when you realize you no longer need to partner-hop to find what's been inside of you all along. When you're pumping a full head of steam from within, the love from another that may then come into your life is grand beyond all expectations, for you're magnetizing to you—if you so desire—a beautiful mirror of your own inner self. Now that's a relationship!

At times, the feelings inside will become so powerful you'll feel you're about to burst. Hello, pituitary gland! Hello, hormone flow! Hello, brain opening up! Hello, awakening! Hello, higher thought! Hello, joy! All because you hugged a bum, or kissed a day, to activate that energy. You're in the flow, you're in alignment, and when you're feeling love, you're being God!

Call forth the feelings. "From the Light of God that I am, I want to love me. So be it." "From the Light of God that I am, help me to be loving and to feel that love moving. So be it." "From the Light of God that I am, I want to feel love so securely within that I'll not care if anyone else loves me but me." (That's when true love comes!)

Keep asking. Practice. Allow it to grow moment to moment. What you've longed for all your life is right inside, waiting to become your greatest treasure. If tears come at any time, allow them and bless them, for in those precious moments you're touching the hem of the God you are, and your electrified soul is recording the milestone for all eternity.

THAT GLORIOUS ADDICTION

Bless every sweet or sour emotion of your past or present. Let them all come. Let them move about you and through you. And while you're asking for feelings, ask for the feeling of your Inner Being to manifest itself in your life. "I want to feel what you are; come forth."

If you're going around in circles, be still and feel what you're feeling. Get out of the chatter of your ego-should's and into the warm bath of emotions from your core. If you're feeling terror, great. At least you're feeling! If you're feeling depression, have a good one. Allow them all, for we learn and grow only through emotion, not through words.

So, learn to feel! Learn to live by intuitive feelings, not by ego-made rules and regulations. Speak well of yourself, pat yourself on the back, be pleased with your progress and with what you are. The inside of you is already divine; what you perceive as you is here to learn, and grow, and feel, and open up to more of its sublime grandness. So give it bravos along the way.

We came here to feel and, once we start, it can become a glorious addiction as we experience the release of our divinity soaring to its true reality. Expression, emotion, tears, laughter, anger, love—let 'em out, let 'em all out, and get into the dance of life. They won't take you over; they'll set you free. If you're afraid of turning this torrent loose, do it anyway. Call Home and allow the help to enfold you. The grandest emotion of all, love, can be yours in a moment if you'll get the channel cleared. You have only to remember you *are* the mind of God here on Earth, feeling, expanding, experiencing. When you truly listen and hear that still small voice inside, what you're feeling is an emotion. What you're hearing is God.

Vive les emotions!

CHAPTER 12
CREATING MIRACLES

Webster defines a miracle as "an extraordinary event manifesting divine intervention in human affairs." Or, "An extremely outstanding or unusual event, thing, or accomplishment." Or, and I love this one, "A divinely natural occurrence that must be learned humanly."

From what I've learned of the grand and simple art of miracle-making, I'll buy all three definitions, particularly since we're all divine. Yet from what we've been taught about miracles, they're supposedly those things only God-out-there knows how to do and most assuredly those things for which we have no plausible explanation. On the contrary, not only are miracles quite easy to explain, their creation is our birthright.

In forgetting our origin, we slipped farther and farther away from that remembrance into the reactive existence of social-consciousness thinking. 'Round and 'round we've gone in that same groove, operating from the limited thinking of those about us, never realizing there was so much more toward which we could stretch our sleeping minds.

Where to work, how to earn, what to wear, what to say, how to act, how to look, when to play, who to love, how to love, what to buy, what to drive, how to live . . . normal, everyday thoughts of social consciousness. We pick them up and send them out, the same mundane thoughts manifesting the same mundane routines day after day, year after year.

The wonder of it is that every one of us was born with the inner power to work miracles. We are all Gods incarnate, birthed into the forgetfulness of human form to press our minds into remembrance. And with that birthing come all the rights of membership in our divinity, including how to make miracles. We have only to put our heads and emotions to work in the sure knowledge and acceptance of this latent—and very divine—capability.

The manifesting of so-called miracles is nothing more than putting into application the principles of consciousness and energy. We pull in a thought of something we want in our life, emotionalize it (get emotional about it) to thrust it back out into the ethers, and release it. If we've embraced the desire totally, and know it exists in that moment, it's got to manifest. We've emotionally shot the units of consciousness out to magnetically draw the item or event to us, or us to it. Cosmic law is in full operation.

Indeed, manifesting is not a fluke. We do it every day but have never known what to call it or how to unleash the power, so we've stayed quite out of control. We've been like fleas frantically hopping around in a bottle who haven't realized the cap was off. Learning the simple steps of manifesting through the principles of consciousness and energy will take us a long way toward turning our lives around, physically, emotionally, intellectually, and spiritually. So! Ready for some life-changing fun? Here we go!

BECOMING THE GENIE

Manifesting, by and of itself, is not a big deal. Nor is it difficult to understand the patterning that brings it about, either daily in mundane routine or in the category of miracles. In the simplest of steps, it goes like this: (1) we want something; (2) we embrace the idea; (3) we get emotional about it (which, most of the time, we're not aware of); (4) we release the idea, knowing it's already in existence; and then, most important of all, (5) we allow it to happen.

Want, embrace, emotionalize, release, allow. None of those actions are awesome or overwhelming. We've been doing them all our lives, in just that order, to get our groceries, or go to a concert. The vital point to remember about manifesting is not to limit our thinking. For those of us on the Program who generally thought that "let go and let God" meant to stand back, get out of the way, and let the chips fall where they may, this means a rather radical change in thinking, for now we're directing where we want the chips to fall.

You suddenly have a yen for a chocolate sundae. There's an ice-cream store nearby, you find change in the dresser drawer, so you go and fulfill that desire. You've just manifested your sundae. Manifesting a new job, new home, or new romance is no different than manifesting the ice-cream sundae; only the time frame may vary according to the energy being directed to activate the circumstance and finally put you into the event.

Look at it this way: any idea that comes to you, or flows from you, is conscious thought. So say you've had this impassioned desire to travel. The thought generates imagination (a high-level God-skill) and the emotion behind it. Together, they start activating the interior thought patterns of electromagnetic consciousness units to create the necessary energy for manifesting. Everything's ready, and out they go

CREATING MIRACLES

into the world to (blurp) change someone's mind, or (blurp) give someone an idea. Like is attracting like. Now, Joe down in the San Juans is hit with an idea which came from you. It matches his particular desires, and (blurp), it's by electromagnetic energy, not coincidence, that he thinks of you. The two energies have met, yours and his, and before you know it, you get a phone call to come speak at an A.A. convention in the San Juan Islands. Bingo! You're traveling.

You can see in that example how your thought to travel went through a search-and-find process. There's nothing unusual about that, for all thoughts attempt to materialize themselves, seeking out the best match of their frequency to become physically translated. And their secret power—indeed the magic wand that makes it all happen—is emotion!

CLEARING FOR TAKEOFF

Imagination and its by-product emotion are two of the most concentrated forms of energy we possess as human beings. In fact, any strong emotion carries more energy with it than, say, what's required to blast a rocket off to the moon. Imagination (thought) sets the juices going (emotion), and to the precise degree you allow yourself to get emotional will that desire come into manifestation. Emotion focuses and fires the energy into the passion of desire. Without it you have wishful thinking, which gets you just that.

Anything that can be envisioned can be brought into physical reality, except money (usually). Money is part of the get-you-there process, so go for what the money will buy, rather than the money itself. If it's a new home, go to work on the style, location, etc., rather than the dollars to purchase it, and before long you'll be selecting the wallpaper.

But first, some honest cleanup is necessary before beginning to exercise this divine right. If, for instance, you strongly believe it will be tough for you to find the job you want because *they* always said you'd never amount to anything, you're blocking the very thing you desire to manifest (better employment) by the power of the internal belief in your subconscious mind. Result? Self-sabotage! The strength of denial is sufficient to magnetically repel the very thing the conscious mind wants to draw.

Let's say you want a totally new kind of relationship. There are two ways you can approach this, but using the two together will get you farther faster. First, do some cleaning up by going inside to ask the Light of God that you are why you've been drawing the same kind of partner-drama to you over and over again. If you've been in a repeat pattern, it's one of your lessons, so be open for the answer.

Next, begin the manifestation process with the internal feeling—and absolute knowingness—that you're changing it this time and going for something better, simply because you deserve it. If you have trouble believing that, call for help until you can believe it with every fiber of your being. Pretend, if you have to. Each time you repeat this process, new neuro-pathways are being woven throughout your brain, allowing the new thoughts to be sent from you with clear, emotional intent. Now, knowing your manifestation is in the process of forming, let go and let God. In other words, let it go and allow it to happen. A new kind of relationship is on its way.

Granted, that approach is quite different from what most of us were taught on the Program. Our saying, "Plan the footwork, but don't plan the results," has been one of our cherished lifesavers. Whatever our problems, it allowed us to walk on with the trust that "it would all work out." While that concept was vitally important in helping us establish a faith, we're now ready to move on. Conscious manifesting requires just the opposite approach. We have to know the results are already accomplished, while staying well clear of trying to arrange the footwork that gets us there. The saying now becomes, "Believe the results, but don't plan the footwork." In other words, we stop trying to push the river upstream.

Another area that will block our ability to consciously manifest our desires is not being in agreement with ourselves. We can't have contradiction going on within us about what we want. "I really want to buy a new car, but I know I'll never be able to afford it." "I really want to go to Hawaii for a month's vacation, but I'll never get that kind of time off." "I want to have free time to paint, but I know the kids come first." There can be no debating, or once again we'll be magnetically repelling with our contradictory beliefs what we want most.

So listen carefully to those feelings or thoughts which follow your statement of desire. If there's a "yeah, but" attached, go to work on it immediately to get yourself into alignment where all of you agrees with this new desire.

"Yes, by God, I *am* worth it." "True, I've never done it before, but I'll find a way." "I've always put everyone else first, now it's time for me," etc. Once you're in agreement, all debating ceases between your God-self and ego-self. "Yep, we agree; so let's go for it." Now nothing can hold back the manifestation except a sluggish fire in your emotional furnace.

Muddy waters always come when you're attempting to manifest from your ego-self and not from your God-self. For example, your best friend was just promoted to vice president of the corporate division and announced at lunch the other day that he'd be moving to a lovely new home in the exclusive hilltop area. Your altered ego says, "Damn, he made it before I did. Oh well, that's OK, I'll just manifest me there." Good luck! Your God-self is saying you're right on schedule where you are for the moment, learning nicely the lessons of this particular plateau. Not-so-deep inside, you really do know it would be rushing things to leapfrog before you're ready. There's no agreement in there, no alignment.

Nonetheless, you go for it. You get emotional to the rafters about living in the executive area, but nothing happens. Your God-self is just sitting back watching you emote, waiting patiently for you to let up so you can get on with your unfinished business—the things you need to complete in the here and now. If you would just stop for a while to go inside and listen to your inner teacher, you would know now is not the time, and save yourself both the emotional effort and the disappointment.

So don't complicate a desire. You'll know when it fits, when it feels right. And when it does, pull out all the stops and go for it with everything in you. That's the only way you're going to learn how to operate the creative tools you've brought into this life. It's the only way you're going to learn of the vast control you have over every moment, every situation, every direction of your life.

Your God-self wants to live, to explore, to be, to enjoy, to sail boats, fly planes, climb mountains, have ten kids, or be president of General Motors. And it wants you to do this because your Book of Life (your soul) is saying that these are experiences still needed for the emotion of them. That's where your lurking desires come from . . . unfulfilled emotions in the soul. So your Inner Being quickly joins forces and says, "Understood, soul, let's press for it." If your altered ego has no fight with the desire, then you're in alignment and have clear sailing ahead to manifest. Just watch for which voice is speaking and don't let that ego-self win out by keeping you victim with "I can't" or "how could I." Take charge into Mastership. You'll know.

Is there, after all, one among us who doesn't want to fill our lives with fullness, honest-to-God love, and happiness? That begins to happen the moment we unleash our emotions in purposeful focus. We become fulltime conscious manifesters, creating our own destiny, living our desires. Who needs three wishes from a magic lamp when we already *are* the genies?

FOCUSING WITHOUT LIMITS

The key to manifesting desires lies in embracing the understanding that everything in your private universe got there through your own emotions! Take, for example, where you live. You probably moved there because you felt emotionally good about it. Or, how about what you wear? You wear what makes you feel good. You go to certain places because you like the way they make you feel, and you eat certain foods, surround yourself with certain people, and do myriads of things simply because they make you feel good. Conversely, those things you once did but didn't like you don't do anymore because you don't like the feelings that go with them.

It's all called experience. Everything you ever did—all the people you drew to you, places you went, problems you had, things you bought—you did for the emotional experience of them. Mostly, that's been unconscious activity. Now you're simply taking yourself off haphazard automatic to *consciously* focus all that unfocused emotional energy into the creation of your desires.

And right here is where you can get hung up. Unless the desire you have is a passionate one, no amount of conscious manifesting in the world will work. You can't get emotionally involved with something you're only halfheartedly interested in. Muddy waters, not-so-hot passion, and lazy self-esteem might combine to get you a mild suggestion of a manifestation, or nothing at all. But deep passion, no blocks, clear intent, and you've got an absolute manifestation working. Your "want" must come to pass, for you've created an emotionally focused desire in your electromagnetic subconscious mind. *Therefore, it now exists in your reality.* You have only to catch up with it in time.

So just remember, your manifestation will always match your emotion, *not the vision* of what you want. It won't match wishful thinking; it will only match your strong emotional reaction to having it.

The importance of manifesting is twofold, really. First, it makes you aware of your own powers and puts you into absolute control of your life.

Second, and by far the most important, each manifestation you are aware of causing (and it's wise to be consciously aware of each one as it comes) activates the awakening process (opening the pituitary, entrance of unlimited thoughts, etc.), thereby quickening your spiral back to your Godhood remembered. You'll feel differently, act differently, see things differently, and attract very differently.

Few people, however, are aware of how limiting their thinking is, even for the things they most deeply desire. So when you start to go down your list of desires to begin the manifestation process, take a long hard look at how narrow your vision may be. Are you manifesting just a new car, when in fact you want a Jaguar? Are you manifesting for just a new home, when in fact you want a five-thousand-square-foot executive mansion overlooking a lake? Are you manifesting to sing in a choir, when in fact you want to be the director?

Granted, those may be exaggerations, but the premise can't be said often enough. We are all unlimited beings able to create unlimitedly anything we desire! If you are to gradually expand into *being* unlimited (which you most assuredly can), it behooves you to practice *feeling* in an unlimited way. When you decide you can love yourself enough to have it, no matter how obscure or ridiculous, doors begin to open everywhere you turn.

WANT, EMBRACE, EMOTIONALIZE; OWN, RELEASE, ALLOW

So let's get on with it. How do you do it? If emotional energy is what electromagnetically charges, and then propels the imagined thought into the ethers to draw to you your deepest desires, how do you intentionally get the thoughts out there? The process is much like making love. Let's say, for example, you're ready for some old-fashioned lovemaking. You think about it, like the idea immensely, and arrange to make it happen.

Now, the energy you use to create a fantasy in your mind to bring about sexual arousal is the same type of focused energy you use for manifesting. It's alive, powerful, and very magnetic.

As your emotions become heated in your lovemaking process, so too does your body. Some of this heat is from exertion, yes, but most is from emotional energy. Your imagination is having a hey-day, you're visualizing like Cinerama, the heat builds with the intensity of emotions, and suddenly there's the release which you just manifested out of desire. This is exactly what happens in the process of manifesting.

While it's certainly not necessary, sitting with your body facing North helps to align with the Earth's magnetic poles and generate greater power. You're ready to begin.

1) *You've decided what you want. There's no argument, and it feels right. (Want) You're emotionally drawn to it. If you can't feel it, you don't want it.*

2) *Now start to visualize this desire of yours, and begin to get into what it will feel like when you have it. (Embrace) Create in your mind's eye your fantasy of having it right then and there. Visualize it, enjoy it, play in it, be with it. Let your body become elated with your laughter or your tears of joy, whatever reaction you'd naturally have, for that's what's going to manifest, and your manifestation will only match your level of emotion. It will never match the vision alone.*

3) *The power is now taking form in the subconscious, while the vision is buzzing around in the brain. More and more emotion is being poured in to fuel the original vision. (Emotionalize) You're really getting jazzed, feeling passionate, your body's heating up, your heart's beating faster, and your respiratory system is slowing down.*

4) *You're in total alignment, on a tremendous high. You know without any doubt that your desire is already in existence. (Own) At that moment, you speak deeply from your Inner Being and fervently own the happening. "From the Light of God that I am, I call forth my desire into power, into manifestation, and into law. So be it."*

5) Suddenly the release comes. Your body goes limp; you feel it all over. (Release) Your emotional desire has shot out into the Isness, completed. And there it will sit, waiting for you to allow it in. It's gone into time; it's gone into Law. When your body comes down from its high, take a few deep breaths, relax, and go back into yourself. Feel what you've just done. Feel the completion. Then thank your Inner Being, and pat yourself on the back for a job well done.

6) You've wanted it, embraced it, emotionalized it, and released it. Now, you have one last step, perhaps the most difficult of all, allow it to happen. In fact, now is the time for you to do two things of utmost importance if you truly want your manifestation to come into being. First, don't discuss it with anyone for any reason! And second, leave the details to the universe and your Inner Being. (Allow)

Talking about your manifestation before it occurs pulls power away from your original focus, depleting the energy required to bring it about. This is not a topic to share at meetings, or even with your sponsor. Over and over again I've seen what might have been a great manifestation ruined by people trying to manipulate the circumstances or talk it away. Circumstances will take care of themselves, but you have to allow the energies full rein to run their course into your reality.

Start small when you begin, so you can see results quickly. If you can't get emotionally involved the first couple of times on one desire, go to another until you can feel that peak come. Do it over and over until you get it down pat on one desire. Once you know you've hit it, go on to another one. If your first one hasn't started to happen after quite a while, then, and only then, go back to it.

How would you react if a lifelong dream suddenly appeared right in front of you? That's how to act in your manifesting process, out loud, with gleeful abandon, wonder, gratitude, and boundless joy. Let it build. Feel the energy change all around you. Feel the magnetism grow. Know you are in control. Become the living character in that fantasy as if it were happening in the moment, because in fact, it is! The manifestation is only the aftermath of your original enactment.

Since few of us on the Program could ever list patience on the asset side of our inventories, consider allowing ample time for the manifestation to occur. When it does, honor yourself soundly, for you're waking up to your own divinity. My God, look what you've done! And you're taking control of your own life.

More important, you're fulfilling your purpose to exercise the power within you that will open up that sleeping mind for splendid new thought, fill your being with overwhelming love, and hand you the freedom to design your world according to every desire you've ever had. Isn't that worth waiting for? Be patient; it will all happen in due time.

I've manifested everything from new homes (for which I had no money prior to manifesting), to fun little things like bikes and power lawn mowers (for which I had no money), to dogs, loving friends, answers to problems (by seeing myself in the answer), people to help remove emotional blocks, a new relationship, vacations, financial security, and serenity in abundance. Manifesting is a reliable, guaranteed miracle-maker that will bring you into such feelings of empowerment, you'll become unstoppable as the genie, precisely what your Inner Being had in mind all along.

Want it with a deeply felt desire. *Embrace* it in agreement with your God-self and ego-self. Passionately *emotionalize* the experience of having it. *Own* the reality of its immediate existence. *Release* the emotions to the universe, then silently *allow* it to take form. Once it does, go ahead and shout it to the world. You've earned the right.

Manifesting has to do with choices. It has to do with knowing our lives are no longer blocked and knowing that being blocked is nothing more than a state of mind. If we keep creating choices in consciousness, we can then create them in actuality by manifesting them into reality. Like our lives, manifesting is pure emotion. It's God in action. It's our divine birthright, using the forces of energy we are. Indeed, manifesting is heady power with a sign on it reading, "For Masters Only!"

AFFIRMATIONS: SHORTCUTS TO NEWNESS

In any bookstore today, happily, you'll find shelf after shelf of books on the art of affirmation, including such topics as how to grow rich by reprogramming, how to turn your life around by positive thinking, or how to cure your body with new thoughts. While they rarely explore the scientific principles of consciousness and energy which lie behind this ancient art, they all have their place in expanding consciousness, for every one of them bases its philosophy on the simple act of changing your thinking. In fact, practicing one or two short affirmations was what catapulted me out of pain and into this new way of life.

Affirmations are powerful tools you can use all day long, wherever you are and in whatever you're doing. They take hold of stubborn old trains of subconscious thought to mold new belief patterns in their place.

Your subconscious mind, remember, is a book of law. Only *it* didn't write the laws; you did. If negative emotions have dominated or controlled your conscious mind most of your life, it goes without saying that your subconscious still carries powerful, negative beliefs which are continuing to electromagnetically draw experiences of like vibrations into your body, your home, your business, your relationships, etc. Since the goal is to change those negative thoughts and their subconscious programming, one way to do that is with affirmations.

The key to reprogramming the subconscious is to reprogram it with *truth*. If your subconscious mind sincerely believes a new thing to be true, you have instant reprogramming. We're back to cause and effect, with your subconscious bringing about the goals set by your conscious.

So if you want to reprogram something that deep down you don't really believe, simply find a way to state it that you can accept as true.

For an exaggerated example, your brother bit you when you were two, so you hate men. To attempt to blatantly fly in the face of that well-ensconced belief and affirm, "I love all men," would be an utter waste of time. Your conscious mind wouldn't believe a word of what you're saying, so neither would your subconscious.

Instead, go for something like, "My reality is in the present, not in the past." "The past is gone and has no hold over me." "I'm forming a new belief about my past." "My mind is learning to obey me." Or even, "Shut up! I'm the boss here!" These are statements you can quickly come to believe and therefore speak with conviction to your subconscious, strongly overriding the old programming.

Affirmations need repeating over and over again. Post them up on your wall, on your bathroom mirror, on your desk, on your car dashboard. They're magic when used with determination.

The trick, always, is to find a way to say something so you can believe it (or often enough, until you do!). If you're stuck with knowing how, call Home for help. That imageless being within you is already jumping up and down with divine delight at your desire to change and will be more than eager to rapidly assist you in finding the right combination of words.

Let's say you just experienced a limiting feeling such as being rejected. If you don't want to keep going through that, then quickly make a mental note that you need to come up with a believable thought for this recurring situation. It might be something like, "Rejection is a feeling I create myself." Or, "When I feel rejected, I'm rejecting myself." Or, "I'm worth more than being tossed away, but I'm the one doing the tossing."

Maybe there's the fellow at work who always seems to push your buttons, but you can't avoid being around him. So rather than, "Sam makes me angry," go for, "I seem to make myself mad when I'm around Sam." Or, "I'm on my way to finding out why I allow Sam to push my buttons." Or, "Anger is a bore. I now release it."

An affirmation is always a positive statement, always affirmed in the present tense ("I am" as opposed to "I'm going to . . . .") and must always be believable. And always, always, see it and feel it as completed, just like any manifestation. This is what creates the override process in your subconscious. If you've been conditioned negatively (as we perceive it), you can recondition your subconscious to react from another position, therefore positively (as we perceive it), provided you believe what you're affirming.

Where the manifesting process is usually implemented for physical circumstance, affirmations are generally best suited for mental control, meaning life control. They can be about anything, so take careful stock of your thoughts and see where change is needed.

"Tom annoys me by being late." Switch the focus to yourself to take control with something like, "Tom reminds me what a stickler I've always been for being on time."

"I can't find the answer to my question." Switch to, "The answer is available to me. I release all blocks, and I am willing to receive the answer."

"I am afraid of that." Test something like, "I'm overcoming my fears now." Or, "Fears are only an illusion." Or, "Fear is of my own making, and I am unmaking it now by walking with my Inner Being."

"I have so few friends." Test out, "I love the new friends I'm acquiring." (Notice the victim/Master relationship to each of the pairs of statements.)

"I am learning to . . . ," "I am becoming . . . ," "I am growing to believe that . . . ," "I am coming to enjoy this new . . ." These tenses will ease you into a new belief until it becomes solidified. Then, as soon as you can, drop the "I am learning" or "I am becoming" and switch to "I am!" But don't be premature with this step. Wait until you firmly believe the strong new positions before jumping in with "I am this or that." Otherwise, your efforts will be fruitless for lack of believability.

Wherever there is a lack, there is always a need we develop to fill that lack. (When we lack love of self, just look at all the needs we develop trying to fill that one!) So when you spot a need, go back and figure out what the lack is so you can create the proper affirmation to correct it. If you find, for example, you look for a lot of stroking, something like, "I'm learning to love myself more every day," will be a simple, yet enormously powerful, step towards breaking that victim-type thinking.

If lack of self-worth is an issue, as it is with most of us, say, "I approve of myself," five hundred times a day and watch what happens!

As you become more bold in your affirmations, there may be times when little thoughts jump in with, "This is nonsense! What I'm telling myself is just not so." Lovingly tell those ego thoughts that you're in control here, and they absolutely cannot play those old tapes anymore. "I release you with love and with no regret for your having been with me."

To affirm is to state that it is so. To affirm is to wipe out an old belief by creating a new one which will go out from you to search the universe for a proper fit. To affirm is to be confident of the results, for in this frame of mind, regardless of all evidence to the contrary, you will call to you that which you truly desire. Such is the law of attraction.

SOUGHT THROUGH PRAYER AND MEDITATION . . .

For years, whenever thinking of Step Eleven, and meditation, and how to improve my conscious contact with God as I understood Him, I envisioned myself sitting cross-legged in a self-induced trance, white robes folded uncomfortably about my stiff body, and a sparkling white turban wrapped about my alpha-state head. I bought books on the subject, went to classes and seminars, and accomplished nothing but the conviction that meditation, as such, was not up my alley.

As for prayer, now that was a different matter. My only problem was, when things were going great, prayer was the farthest thing from my mind. When things weren't so hot, I was usually too busy trying to figure my way out of the mess to call on my Higher Power, or too deep into the problem to bother "HP" with it anyway.

Prayer needn't be limited to down on the knees or other formal rites of worship. In fact, each time we invoke the assistance of our Inner Being, "From the Light of God that I am, I call for . . . ," we're praying, reconnecting with the mind of God. This is prayer of the highest vibratory sense, for we're invoking our own divinity to respond, a power which transcends all other energy for humankind.

Prayer is having little chats with the God of our Being as we might chat with an old friend on the phone, and truly, that's not unlike what we're doing. Each time we so much as think God, we're putting in a call to—and connecting with—the Source, as well as our Inner Being. They're on the same party line. Call one, you get the whole.

There's no right or wrong to prayer; the point is to get in the habit of doing it until it becomes a part of every waking moment, for in its truest sense, prayer is nothing more than hooking into God-consciousness by expanding our own consciousness. The more we do it, the faster our entire body frequency changes, building on its own momentum, frequency by frequency. Negative thoughts dissolve more rapidly, manifestations begin to show up, answers click in, our knowingness expands, and our subconscious minds start picking up topics for affirmations as though we were reading them off a grocery list! All this from sending thoughts Home on wings of love as often as we think of it throughout the day.

Now, prayer and meditation are the same in principle but different in application. Unlike my vision of having to sit cross-legged contemplating my navel, meditation can be almost anything that causes us to silence the jabbering intellect and focus into the joy of beingness.

We all need to find times to just be, whether experiencing the quietude of music, sitting on a beach or under a tree, walking nature's paths, dining in simple splendor, watching flames dance in the fireplace, thinking by candlelight, or just holding hands with a loved one. Such times of quiet are not easy for us "keep-everything-moving-and-filled-with-activity-so-I-don't-have-to-think" Twelve-Steppers. I well remember my first five minutes of enforced quiet, like which part of me was going to explode first, my head or my whole body? I could sit for hours listening to flamboyant opera, or watching TV, or reading a book, but just sit and do nothing? Whoa!

Actually, those times of high quiet come to be times of high joy. They're times when we open doors to walk into a broader Light, into a wider sense of what we are. Such times move us beyond our intellect to reach our center, the frequency of our own divinity. In truth, this kind of meditation, or contemplation, is the path to releasing those deeply buried treasures of self-love we all hold within us. That alone would be enough reason to pursue a few moments of daily quiet, a small price to pay for learning unconditional love of self.

Give it a try. Sit for a few moments in nature's lap, or on your front porch, or in your favorite armchair, and just be. In those moments you're without judgments, worries, or fears. For a few precious moments you touch your true identity, pure love, and find yourself in an unfamiliar state of contentment and peace. In those moments, you are living your God, not your image.

In the silence of contemplation, your brain waves actually soften, allowing higher thought a much easier time coming through. Those are the times to listen carefully to what may be popping into your head, those little "aha's" that are your creative jewels. Those moments of, "Wow, great idea!" What you're hearing is purposeful, so never doubt it. It's cosmic mind, uni-mind, God-mind, your own higher thought being pulled in by your soul with something you need to hear. It's your intuition, a vision, a neat thought, an outrageous idea. Don't doubt those thoughts! You've tuned in to another frequency and now have an entire universe on your new wavelength. You needn't strain to hear, just let the thoughts in without negating their origin, authenticity, or sanity. The universe will whisper its secrets to you if you're open and willing to receive.

WHEN PRAYERS ARE HEARD

And now, if you've ever wondered (and haven't we all) if your prayers are heard, the answer is an unequivocal "Yes!" From different levels of frequency, and from different dimensions, we are all heard, and helped, and loved. So never be too proud to pray, even if it's just, "Thanks," or a few mental thoughts of gratitude to your Higher Power within and without. Every word, every thought, is heard.

And how should you pray? Who cares, so long as you do it all day long, in little thoughts here and there, until it's a habitual part of your life. Just as on the Program there are no "should's, or "how to's." The only difference between right or wrong prayer is whether you're doing it with your heart or with your head.

If it's by rote, you'll be heard, but nothing much will happen. If it's from your heart, where you can feel the vibration setting up, you'll be heard. If you really get into it with some grand emotion,

you'll be heard throughout the universe. If, however, you mix gratitude with that emotion, your prayer will be heard throughout the
omniverse, for there is no time or distance to the thought waves of
deeply reverent prayer.

Prayer not only goes out, it goes within. At night, ask your Inner
Being what troubles you, and ask the trouble to come forward so that
you might deal with it. Then finish with a moment of reverence, and
you've set your body to receive higher consciousness flow throughout the night. Powerful help is available for your subconscious in
that manner, and you'll recognize the forthcoming help in the form
of new awarenesses throughout the days to follow.

Asking for joy is prayer. For instance, in the quiet of the morning hours in bed, ask for joy to be with you that day. Ask for love to
be with you. You deserve it, so ask for it. Then know from the core of
your being that joy will be there, and it will, no matter what may be
going on about you.

Asking for direction is prayer. Asking to expand is prayer. Asking
for knowledge, for understanding, for enlightenment, for higher
consciousness, for love, is all prayer. Asking in prayer changes your
energy, particularly when you put your awareness into your heart
center and feel the depth of your request.

So ask for love, ask for compassion, and peace, and happiness.
Then become a listener as you have never listened before in your life.
Listen with an excited expectation, an anticipation, and from the
depths of your soul know you will hear an answer when it's time.

That idea, that new little thought, that feeling, that person, that
happening, they're all answers to prayers, those wonderful non-
coincidences that will fill your day with validations if you'll be
watchful for them. Our Program expression, "Coincidence is a
strange way to spell God," couldn't be more right, for indeed,

coincidences don't exist; they are only answers to prayers, or lessons to be learned.

Indeed, help from the universe is more abundant now than ever before in recorded or unrecorded histories. Never has there been such a time to ask for help, for never has there been such a gathering of grand, loving energies ready and eager to assist.

But remember, universal law is the law of free will, honored and respected without question throughout the cosmos in reverence for life. Because of free will, assistance can only come when you call. So if you want help, say sincerely, "Please help me." That is a prayer heard, and always answered.

And then perhaps, in a thoughtful mood one night you go outside and in meditative prayer look up into forever and ask, as I did, "Inner Being, what have I really learned? What am I really doing? Is all this taking me someplace?" And you fidget, and wonder, and doubt, and think that since you haven't seen angels or heard heavenly choirs, you've somehow failed.

Through all the doubts, the prayers of that moment raise your frequency. Answers begin to flow through you in a kind of knowingness, not in words, but in feelings. And the feelings say, "Oh yes, something in me is different."

As the knowingness speaks from your soul, you realize in that sublime, precious moment that the something different in you is real, is growing, is forever, and is sweet beyond words.

And so you go back inside with a quietness unknown to you before, a sureness of direction, a serenity founded on divine solid rock, though your whole world may be falling apart at the seams. It was one of those times, one of those never-to-be-forgotten moments. You were made quite new that night by nothing but thought and emotion, another miracle, born of prayer.

CHAPTER 13

LIVING YOUR TRUTH

Most of us with any time on the Program will generally agree the Twelve Steps, that great legacy of Bill W. and Doctor Bob, were divinely inspired. So great has been their impact on humanity, it could be said the entire direction of the world today, in its heightened awareness of spiritual values, has come from the tenets of these beloved steps which have guided untold millions in every corner of the world into new life.

Going beyond the Twelve Steps does not mean leaving them behind. It cannot, for those steps have been (and still are) our life, the foundation of everything we hold dear and sacred. Going beyond simply means taking all we have gained from the steps with us, continuing to utilize those principles in all our affairs, and moving quietly into a greater expansion of those principles we so highly revere.

There are few thoughts in this book that are not in some way spoken to, implied, or referred to in one form or another in our Big Book. We've simply allowed ourselves to lose some of the original beauty and intent of the Big Book by becoming caught up in the focus of mass consciousness, the God-out-there syndrome. While our Higher Power has served us magnificently in our growth to date, for those of us who have felt that call for greater expansion in our Program, we see these apparently new concepts as nothing more than a gentle refocusing to our God within.

So we begin to implement what may appear to be a new way of thinking. And yet how new is it? In the chapter "Into Action" from our Big Book we have the promises of the Program. "The spiritual life is not a theory. . . . We are going to know a new freedom and a new happiness. We will not regret the past nor wish to shut the door on it. We will comprehend the word serenity and we will know peace. . . . That feeling of uselessness and self-pity will disappear. . . . Our whole attitude and outlook upon life will change. Fear of people and of economic insecurity will leave us. We will intuitively know how to handle situations which used to baffle us. We will suddenly realize that God is doing for us what we could not do for ourselves. . . . To some extent we have become God-conscious. . . . But we must go further . . ." (Alcoholics Anonymous 1975, 83-85).

Now we are going further, by turning our focus away from separation—God there, me here—to the oneness of which we are a part. We're turning inward, perhaps for the first time in our lives, to hear the voice of our own divinity.

There's no formula for this path, just one day at a time, one foot in front of the other on ancient but long-forgotten ground. With each step comes greater trust, greater joy, and excitement as we begin to live the truth of our reality. And there's no hurry, just passion and desire.

Then comes the leap of faith. We begin to trust what we hear, and that it's not made up. We tune into our intuition and trust it. We allow thoughts to come to us that will light our path to joy.

We face our limitations, embrace them, begin to master them. We let go of guilt and judgment and all things that keep us from knowing the totality of the God we are. We face our fears and strip them down to their illusions.

The things we've longed for, we go and do. And when times seem tough, we know from the God we are that everything's going in the right direction. We're living our truth.

Our absolute birthright is to create a life that makes us happy. Indeed, we can become whatever we desire to become when we've given ourselves permission to do that and reach down for the truth that says we're worth it.

So slow down and live in the moment. Start speaking highly of yourself. Become your own ideal rather than someone else's. Claim your birthright to a life of joy. And then, know that you are forever. Know there is no end to anything.

Those of us who have embarked upon this journey have found not only an unimagined freedom of life but a reason for being that stretches beyond thought. Every day takes on a new quality, a sort of glorious anticipation as we peel away our carefully constructed images and walk deeper into the reality of who and what we are.

If you want what's offered on this platter of bountiful life, and are willing to go to any lengths to get it, this is the process that has worked so miraculously for us.

A FEW GENTLE REMINDERS

We're not alone in this vast consciousness called space. Help is all about us in the unseen, loving us, cheering us on, whispering (sometimes shouting) messages, gently sending forth assistance when we put in a call, standing beside us always. We have no idea how great the strength that walks with us, nor how deep the love that surrounds us, far beyond our understanding of the word.

Yet in all of the loving unseen there is no voice that will teach us greater than our own, for that part of the mind in which truth abides is in constant communication with the All In All, whether we choose to be aware of it or not. Never for a moment does our teacher leave our side. Never for a moment does our soul neglect our daily bread.

When we were youngsters and took a little tumble, we yearned for the nurturing and gentle reassurance of Mom or Dad and to be told all would be well. Some of us got that reassurance; many of us did not. Now when we find ourselves longing for that same warm comfort, we need only remember how much love there is wrapped about us and within us, a force beyond our comprehension which is there to hold us, protect us, guide us ever so patiently along our path Home. That force is there when we tumble, when we hurt, or when we win a race; we have only to *know* that it is.

"We came, we came to, we came to believe" in that loving guidance, with practice. And this kind of practice is the easiest yet, for it takes only a moment's thought, and you're practicing.

As you practice feeling that love, you come to know the God you are. Or, as you practice feeling God, you come to know the love. Practice as you lie in bed at night, in the morning, on the way to work, on a private walk, or under a tree. Practice knowing you're held in the hand of the God you are and totally loved. When that love is acknowledged, the circuit is completed, and you brush against Creation . . . moments impossible to describe.

It's the "fix," the feeding of that deep hunger, the realization that you and God are one, and that you are not now, never have been, and never will be, alone. That loving, supportive energy has always been there. All you need do is believe it, use it, and not wait for proof. If you've been in deep stress, you've been in a deep-freeze, so you reach for the warmth and allow the energy of your own being to slowly thaw you out. You *feel* again and start living.

When you call on the Power to do what it brought you here to do, you have instant attention, instant nurturing, instant love, instant thought in action. Just by thinking about it and feeling it (or pretending to feel it at first), you've connected.

So when you're afraid, or sitting in the midst of turmoil, quietly call on that Power and say, "I want to experience the peace of my Inner Being, now!" Feel your desire, for that's the trigger that will shoot you and your fear right to your God-center where you can operate from strength rather than from a stressed-out image.

You're not creating this connection, nor is it just your imagination; it's already there. You're merely activating it through consciousness by turning your awareness deep within. Once the connection is made, the peace and strength in the midst of turmoil comes with ease.

There'll be bumps along your way, sure. You're going to go through fires, those lessons yet to be learned. Everyone on this path has been through them. And if you want to be true to your course, you'll call for more fires, more lessons, more of whatever it is you came here to learn, and each time you'll find you come out on the other side because you've learned to raise your consciousness to a frequency where problems find solutions.

Many times, oh, how many times we wanted to say, "To hell with it all. It's too painful. It's too hard. It's asking too much." But then, because we had called for help, we could sense that loving voice within saying, "Little one, you do not stand alone against the world. You stand with Me, for you are not a singular person; you are My original thought. You are the Light of what I am. You are the Light of God." Comforted and heartened, we moved on.

LIVING YOUR GOD, BEING YOUR JOY

The happiest people I know who are walking this road to remembrance make a deliberate habit of living their truth. They made a conscious decision to come out of the pain and be happy, period. It didn't happen by luck; they simply decided "enough!" of the joyless life. No more living for the expectations of others and all the accompanying "should's." They made a conscious decision to go full steam into loving themselves and gracefully allow everyone else to do whatever it is they need to do. They make a point of laughing a lot just to raise their frequencies. They find what gives them joy in their lives and go for it. They're living from and through their God, narrowing that margin of separation from one day to the next.

When you get to the point of knowing (and it may be this afternoon, or next year) that you and God are one, you've removed separateness from your thought process and literally united with the Godhead once again. Even if you're not yet totally remembering, the reunion's taken place, and you've opened the doors to a world of unlimited possibilities.

As you begin to experience more and more of this power, see if you can live *from* it, or off of it. As a flower lives off the nutrients from the soil, air, and sun, you can learn to live from the God of your Being. Allow it to step in and be you, to take over, to react through you, to feel through you, to melt your image and look through your eyes into the God of another to see only that God, not the man-made outer self.

As you do this, you'll find your awareness of even the littlest things to be so different it may astound you. "My God, I never used to think like that!" "Why, I can't believe that what he said didn't bother me." "I handled the situation with such ease, it amazed me!"

And so you bridge the gap to that awareness that you and God are One, and everything begins to change in quantum leaps. You see all people, places, and things in a different light, not because you think you "should," like "little goody-two-shoes," but because you're allowing yourself to see through the eyes of your God-self. Each time you do, each time you really feel it's happening, you're closing the gap even more. Separation, and the emptiness it breeds, is taking a back seat to joy. And what is joy but God expressing through you?

"I choose to let my God-self express through me today." And the label might read, *"Warning! This trip will prove hazardous to your misery!"*

THE JOY LIST

I've not talked a lot about joy, for it's an emotion foreign to most of us. Yet it's so totally a part of where we're going that to gloss over it is like hiding the pot of gold at the end of the rainbow.

We all know what we think joy is, but here are some little-known extras. To begin with, we can swing into joy as fast as it takes to think about it. If you don't believe that's possible, think about the one million dollars you just won in the sweepstakes. Now dive into that feeling. Pretty nice, isn't it? (Or, are you thinking, "Oh, how ridiculous, that could never happen to me!?")

Why do you suppose joy makes you feel so good? Is it because what you're thinking about is nice, like that one million dollars? If that's so, what makes that thought "nice"? Or is it because the feeling of joy momentarily removes you from pain or boredom? And if that's so, why does just switching your thought pattern (and wasn't it easy?) from glum to giddy make you feel so wonderful?

The reason is simple. Joy is high energy that can exist only in the now, not yesterday, not tomorrow. Since the only place your God can live through you is in the now, when you're into joy you're living one hundred percent through your God-self!

Joy, therefore, is immense power in action, and like love, the highest vibration there is. Joy and its partner, love, are of the same frequency. When we allow it to permeate us, the high vibrations create the physical and emotional sensations we so relish, catapulting us right out of our slow, social-consciousness vibes of yesterday and tomorrow, smack into love, spelled N-O-W.

That doesn't mean we have to be higher than a kite all day long. It means only to be aware that we have a choice of frequencies from which to operate. Joy is a natural ingredient of life if we would only loosen up and allow it to be there.

Let's say you have turmoil (pain) in your life because of your relationship, so you're living in that low vibration, pulling in only thoughts of need and want . . . and pain. And of course the more you focus on it, the more you pull in, and the more you pull in, the greater the pain. Hello, turmoil!

So now you make a simple decision (not necessarily to get rid of all the pain right now, since that might be too involved) to raise your frequency any way you can think of doing it. That will at least give you some relief to think more clearly, maybe even get you some answers.

So let's see . . . what raises frequency? "Well, asking for help does. Good, I'll do that. OK, and meditation of some sort does. Great! And well, working on manifesting does." Terrific, you're on a roll!

What else? "Well, thinking about sending love to someone through a hug will work too, won't it?" Super, what else? "Well, maybe for now I'll just call for more help. That seems to be the easiest." Hey, go for it; now how do you feel? "Wow, much better."

Raise your frequency any way you can, and the death of those low frequencies is certain. You'll walk right out of the problem and into the high vibration of joy, where you can pull in solutions to whatever's going on.

Remember, you can't solve a problem in the same frequency in which it was created. Change the frequency; solve the problem.

Joy doesn't mean shouting at the top of your lungs or winning the sweepstakes. It's a vibrational place you can stay, and be, until that staying becomes second nature. Joy is knowing you're in the process of change. Joy is making a decision to live for you and be happy. And how long does it take to become happy? Just long enough to think joy, and you begin to smile.

Joy is an energy of such power that if you were to live in its vibration steadily for twenty-one days, you'd actually become that vibration, permanently! *That* is what it would be like to be all the way Home, all power, all Light, all love, all joy. God, man/woman, realized!

But for most of us, joy has been only an occasional caller, mostly because we never realized it could be ours on a more permanent basis. Here it is, the magic frequency that releases our belief in the need for struggle, brings absolute, unconditional love of self (the greatest love we can have) along with the absolute freedom which comes from that love, and most of us are still wondering how we get it!

Raising frequencies is nice, but isn't there something more concrete, something we could really get our teeth into without all this "airy-fairy" business? Yes, there is, a tool so simple its power defies imagination. That tool is a "joy list."

Few of us have the foggiest idea what makes us happy. We could sit down and list with the greatest of ease all those things we dislike, but to focus on what gives us joy on a day-to-day basis, well, who's ever thought of it?

And yet we each have those small joys, little things that bring us enormous pleasure and contentment. By listing those simple pleasures and adding to the list as often as new ones pop into our thoughts, we begin to switch the focus of our attention. Unconsciously, we begin to do what we've reminded ourselves we like to do. Voila! Instant joy-making!

My first attempt at a joy list was astonishingly meager. In fact, it was downright difficult. I found myself listing big, major things that could only happen once in a blue moon, like going to a favorite opera, or sailing on a lake at sunrise. It appeared there was little in my life that gave me joy, and the shock was discouraging.

Gradually, though, I got in the swing of it and started to push for day-do-day possibilities, little things I loved doing (or having) but rarely thought about. Taking time to read, having clean dogs, having friends for dinner, doing my hair, taking a long shower, making mashed potatoes, watching the stars, fiddling at the piano, smelling fresh-ground coffee.

To my astonishment, the list started to flow from me like water from a jug. From a list of six or seven, there eventually grew pages of activities that give me joy. Each moment another one would pop into my head, I'd jot it down on whatever was handy (and I still do), a match cover, a restaurant napkin, then transfer it to my permanent list at home.

The teaching in this simple process speaks for itself. As we focus our attention on those pleasures in which we so delight, and reinforce that attention by looking frequently at our lists, we automatically begin to do them. Day by day we increase the moments of joy in our life, casting aside a "should" here, or a chore there, for something from our magic list. We begin to think about joy, what it means to us, and how little it really takes to bring that feeling about. And while we don't neglect the big ones, such as climbing Mt. Everest, our focus is on the obtainable nows, those sweet moments of pleasure we so love, but rarely allow, or even remember. With our joy list, we remember, and we do.

So ask yourself what makes you happy, put it on your list, and do it! The more moments you spend being happy and living in that frequency, the more you are gathering your moments into the now where joy is and God lives.

BECOMING LIFE

When it's all falling down around you, and you can't seem to find the door to get inside, and even your cosmic telephone seems to be unplugged, take your body outside and find life. There is no greater instant turnaround than the vibrations of nature, and the farther away you can get from crowds with their consistently low frequencies, the better.

Getting out into nature cleanses, yes, but more important, it reminds us of life and our enormous desire to live it. Nature reaches back into our soul memory and says, "Hello in there. Remember when we were on the same wavelength? Remember when we could talk to each other? Remember when you could hold me in your hands and feel my love and vibrations? Well, even though *you're* asleep, I'm not. Let me in, and I'll help you change your vibrations! I'll help you to feel again."

If you can get away for a full week by yourself, you'll be transformed. If you have only a few hours, grab them with gusto. If you have an opportunity to sit in the middle of a field during a raging storm, do it, and live every splendid moment of it. If you can get up before sunrise and watch the splendor of the birthing sky become rose, and gold, and white fire, do it, and feel it. If you can sit by a brook and feel its total allowance of all that you are as it moves its own consciousness into the oceans of time, do it, and thank it.

Nature allows, and we need that allowance desperately at times. Nature doesn't judge; it just loves. It lets us feel our aliveness, and if we extend the invitation, it will always reach in to fire up the spark we sometimes think has gone out.

Look at nature with a different eye and listen to its lessons. What does the tree know that you don't? What secrets does the ant hold that you've forgotten? And what does the caterpillar tell you of the changes that lie ahead?

Watch a squirrel scurry along a branch and find your laughter. Feel the power of a wave and listen to its success. The sun will never curse you, and the moon will never say you must be this way or that. The wind will play with you for as long as you want, as often as you want, and the snow in its silence will fill you with high vibrations of peace.

In nature, because you're breathing in all that is about you, you become that consciousness for brief moments of quiet joy. And in that becoming, you change for a little while. You find strength to plug into the universe for feelings, for answers, for help, for love, for understanding, for whatever it is you are needing. From that quiet space you'll be heard.

And then play with your thoughts. Place a thought on a bobbing leaf as it rides by in the stream. Send a thought to the sun. Talk with a tree. Concentrate on a baby cloud and watch it dissipate back into forever. Let your thoughts go wild. Unleash them and push them out of their corral.

Then go even farther. Don't just place a thought on the sun . . . go to the sun! Don't just talk to the tree; become the tree. Feel what it's like to be the grass or a blossoming flower. What's it like to be an ancient snow-capped mountain? Get yourself up there with a seagull or into a worm-pull with a robin. Be the heat of a campfire. Dance in the void between stars. Go sit on a nebula. Become the wind and blow the leaves, or the baby's ball, or the ripples on the lakeshore. Become nature! Become one with life; it's what you are!

As you return home, feel your newness and *stay in that high vibration for as long as you can.* Then go out tomorrow, if possible, and the next tomorrow, and the next. Each time you do, let your imagination go out farther and farther. Give it full rein; let it have its head. Play with it. Talk to nature, laugh with her, become her. Become the black night. Become the void. Become original thought. Let the tears come. Go back to the Light. Become the God that you are. Feel what God's like. Become one with everything you see or hear. Meld with it. Become the "I Am." Speak to forever. "I Am!" It is the prayer of eternity. Nothing about you will ever be the same.

KEYS TO THE KINGDOM

Though I know each path is a singular one, how I wish I could reach out and take your hand so we might travel this road together. And how I would love to share in the joy that lies just ahead of you, those precious moments of discovery, and awe, and happiness, and tears.

A new world is before you, if you will allow it. Be open to your truth and living it. Let your feelings be your guide. At every turn, remember that there is always a happier way. Let in the thoughts that will take you there. Do away with those things in your world that prevent you from knowing the totality of what you are.

Learn to feel, and learn to call those feelings forth from your soul memory, for they are indeed the keys to the kingdom of heaven. To know God completely is to feel every thought completely, until every thought that God is, you are.

Know to the greatest depths within you that we each create our lives through that magnificent inner power, the Source which will never leave us; it is what we are. Learn to honor that Source, and to move, and speak, and act through the Godliness of that Source— You.

And then early one morning when the world is yet dark, and stillness lies on the great Earth, you may feel an urge to rise from your bed and sit by the cool dampness of the window. You won't know why, but you will. All about you is in preparation for the day's newness. The birds have wakened, the moon is gone, and one by one the stars go out as a deep purple hue stretches across the sky.

As you're caught up in the awesome splendor of dawn's unfolding drama, you realize you've momentarily forgotten your cares. You've allowed yourself to become one with the ongoingness of life. You've become the trees, now silhouetted against the brightening horizon. You've become the orange in the sky, the dew on the sill, and the song of the bird. You have become Life itself, the All In All, the Source, your Inner Being, God. You have become Unlimited Thought.

There is no more searching, no more pain or confusion, no more dismay, no more loneliness. There is only truth. You have become your truth, because you are living it. There is no more darkness; there is only Light.

That morning is waiting to come for each of us. It will come for you, if you want it.

EPILOGUE

MY STORY

What is it that motivates some of us to open up to that deep longing within? Well, what did it take to get us to the Program and stop an addiction? It's the same thing really, pain. Only one kind is of the mind and body, while the other is of the soul and spirit.

True, we say that addictions are spiritual as well as physical. But though I remained quite sober for more than two decades before embarking on this amazing journey, and though my sobriety was looked upon as "good Program," if I could count the grains of sand on the shore, they might equal the number of times I had yearned to realize my oneness with God, most of the time quite unconsciously.

"Good Program" or no, that hunger inside for something more won't be stilled until finally it can no longer be ignored. While the emptiness, or longing, might not be the same kind of pain we experienced before joining the Program, it is no less intense. Mix the internal longing with a large dose of emotional pain, and Boom!

Something goes off inside, shouting, "Enough already! I give up! Show me what's missing! I want some answers!" That's what happened to me.

It took years of planned wandering—sometimes sober, sometimes only dry—and more blood-curdling and totally unnecessary crises than I care to think about to get me to that High Sierra lake where it all started for me. There, for the first time in my life, I felt I was a part of, not separate from, that "power greater than myself." Sure, I felt "a part of" when I joined A.A., but I don't remember ever feeling a part of life until those days at my lake.

When I moved from New Jersey to Hollywood in my early thirties, it was a move of terror. Something told me it was well past time to leave the family ties (which also included some rampant alcoholism), but venturing away from my safe and secure sandbox where I knew exactly how, when, where, and with whom to drink my martinis—in or out of New York City—was a leap of fearful faith. Nonetheless, my restlessness won out and before I knew it, I was ensconced in a plush, swinging singles' apartment, smack in the middle of Glitterville.

About one year of that life was all my very alcoholic self could handle. After reaching the rather curious bottom of drinking only in gas stations, or in the ladies' room of the posh Beverly Hills corporate office where I was (barely) employed, I just gave up one day and headed for my first A.A. meeting in downtown Hollywood.

Getting sober in Los Angeles has to be an alcoholic's dream. Even at that time, in the early sixties, there were over six hundred meetings a week in the area, and it was almost all hard-core. You came to believe in a Higher Power, or you were told quite explicitly how and why you weren't going to make it, along with story after hairy story to prove the point.

So I did come to believe, and sincerely so. God was as much a part of my everyday thinking as was my desire to stay sober and grow. I was "willing to go to any lengths," and if that meant seven to ten meetings a week, with two spiritual meetings tossed in on Sunday because my sponsor said so, then fine. I went willingly.

With absolute trust in my Higher Power, a couple of years on the Program, and not the faintest idea what I was doing, I launched a national audio-visual educational publishing company. It was at once the joy and the terror of my life, for while I thrived on the creativity necessary to bring product to a national market, my need to be in absolute control began to erode that precious spiritual bond I had so lovingly woven with my Higher Power. You might say we didn't see eye to eye, my HP and I. I wanted it *this* way, while my Higher Power always seemed to want it *that* way. The impasse remained, and the separation grew, though I never realized for one moment what was happening. While I spoke "Higher Power" from the podium, I lived in a growing aloneness from that power.

I sold the business after almost a decade of developing the company into a front-runner. It was by then as well known as I was worn out, on all fronts. The same fear of not being in control that had so tormented me in business was now plaguing me in every area of my life, including personal, though I truly didn't know it.

Moving to a huge house in the Los Angeles suburbs overlooking the majestic San Gabriel mountains didn't do it. Taking a trial run at different New Thought churches didn't do it. A five-year "geographic" to a picturesque, little oceanside town with a spectacular, oceanview home didn't do it. Trying to live my personal life through Pollyanna, rose-colored glasses didn't do it. I was a frantic mess, and I didn't want to know it. Nothing was working. I was going nowhere, accomplishing nothing, and, with some twenty-three years on A.A., enjoying very little of the journey.

When the breakup came, I had so conditioned myself to believing that everything was fine in all areas of my life, the devastation was immediate and overwhelming. I tried to turn to my Higher Power, but no matter how hard I looked, or where, I could make only mediocre contact, not nearly enough to sustain the weight of my pain.

If there was a bookstore within ten miles of my home back in Los Angeles, I was in it, buying everything I could put my hands on that had to do with "getting over addictions to people," "getting lovers back," "healing from the divorce," etc., etc. Not one book had to do with the real source of my pain, the total separation from my God-self. Of course, even if I had seen such a book, I would only have laughed at its obvious stupidity.

Until we put out the call, we're left alone. But once that call for help goes out, no matter how fragile the voice, help will come if the plea is sincere. My pain was not just from a breakup; it was from a life of spiritual starvation and phony happiness. No matter how deep my belief in a Higher Power, there was always something missing that I just couldn't put my finger on (and never much cared to think about).

But now I was falling off the cliff. I didn't care who or what was listening; I needed help fast. Again and again I'd wake up in a cold sweat in the middle of the night and find myself on my knees beside the bed uttering from the unknown depths of my being—and perhaps for the first time in my life with unqualified sincerity—"Help me. Please help me!" The calls went out, and help came almost immediately, though I surely didn't see it as divine intervention at the time.

Unusual meetings I'd never before attended, strangers suggesting a supplementary new Program, a church that was new to me, a chance opening in an ACOA Program workshop, a book that appealed to my intellectualism, a vacation I would never have thought of taking, along with the appearance of a little money from nowhere to help it along, and lakes that in my wildest dreams I could not have conjured up to so perfectly meet my longing for upliftment; they came together in flawless orchestration to offer help. Now it was up to me.

Pain had put only a temporary cover on my deeply hidden hunger. Bit by bit, the messages from that little book I had taken to the lake on how to use the laws of mind started ringing bells in my soul. Day after day in that breathtaking setting, with not a body around, I devoured its simple message that we are the directors of our own fate through the nature of our thoughts, that we give our peace away by surrendering control over our thoughts, and that prayer in any form is also communion with the indwelling God, the living spirit which is the reality of every person.

The day before I left my precious lake, where I had arrived only a week before in anguish and turmoil, I knew my life had changed. I wasn't sure how as yet, but I knew it in every fiber of my being. And I knew something else; if it was this easy for me to change gut-wrenching pain to love and peace with only a few simple affirmations out of a funny little book, I would find out more about this way of thinking and pass it on to any Program person who might have the same longings. Somehow, some way, that was to be my life from that day forward.

Little did I know how swiftly the energies of the universe unite to take you up on your desires to awaken. Suddenly I was enrolled in school to complete my doctoral degree in Behavioral Science. While

I was up to my ears in that program, and still keeping a mortgage company going, I enrolled in the first year course toward ministry in The Church of Religious Science (also known as Science of Mind). I began to attend seminars by masters of high spiritual learning. Very few books on the esoteric sciences, and very few of the great teachers from other realms, escaped my insatiable hunger. I just couldn't get enough of it all. My life had done a one-eighty, and I wanted more, more, more, *now!*

An abundance of money started coming into my life for the first time, and with good reason. Old beliefs were shaking loose, my victim mentality was turning around, and I was happy. There was a lilt to my step and a gleam in my eye. I loved going to A.A. meetings more than ever, and I also loved my time alone more than ever. Something was coming alive inside of me; something was waking up; something was taking hold of me and saying, "Well, hello there . . . it's about time! Welcome to the start of an amazing new life."

The more I studied these universal truths which so fully answered the age-old questions of who we are, where we've come from, what we're doing here, and why, the more it became clear that all the great masters, including my own personal teachers, were saying precisely the same thing. Some would couch their teachings in language of old, others in more modern-day verbiage, but not one variance ever occurred in the main themes regarding our own divinity, our oneness with all that is, thought, Light, energy, the Source, our soul, our reason for being here, creation, evolution, and so on. Their words would resonate throughout my being so forcefully and emotionally that at times they'd literally take my breath away. And again, I'd want more.

After I pushed and urged, my doctoral committee finally allowed me to do my dissertation on "The Physics of Thought."

Since in their minds there could be no such thing, as physics was the study of what was known, not unknown, they agreed most reluctantly and with ponderous qualifications. That was fine with me; I was thrilled they'd given in and would allow me to present an empirical—though somewhat unorthodox—study on the nature of thought.

Those months I call my "dissertation year" were among the happiest of my life. Each piece of new evidence seemed to fit with perfect alignment into the puzzle we call consciousness, and everything I was learning for my degree was, in turn, creating a major change in my own life.

Sometimes at night, after coming home from an A.A. or ACOA meeting, I'd sit in my living room with the lights out, thinking about all that had happened in the last few months, and would suddenly feel washed with joy, and gratitude, and body warmth. I know now that was the energy of my own God within expressing, but it was wonder and newness to me then.

Or I'd be standing at the sink doing dishes, thinking about my connection to the Source, when all of a sudden my little cockapoo would start yapping at me, obviously frightened of something. At the same time, one of "those feelings" would be sweeping over me where I'd feel in love with all mankind, not to mention my own Self. I know now my little dog was seeing what I felt, the Light of my Being on fire from the joy of my thoughts.

Today, there's not a day I don't engage in some way at calling forth my Light. The hunger for that Light is so strong that at times I wonder why I'm not literally on fire.

Neither is there a day I don't in some way bump heads with my image. Ah yes, that grand old ego is still playing its devious games, only now it takes just a day or two (sometimes only a few moments) rather than years to realize what's happening. So loud is the voice from my Inner Being to burn away that shell, rarely a day goes by I don't call Home to bring on whatever the unfinished ego-business of my life may be, no matter the discomfort. Granted, it's not always pleasant, but as long as I remember everything's on course and call Home for help, each crazy circumstance, or challenge, becomes another battle won in getting closer to my own reality.

The wonderful difference in my life now is that I know where I'm going and how to get there. No matter what the adventures may be, no matter how many bumps or roadblocks, no matter those chunks of unmelted ego, and no matter the lessons, there's an indescribable joy in my being that says, "Thanks, you grand Light, for finally getting through to me. Show me the road to the God I am, and let's go Home."

From the depths of my being, I pray this, too, will become your passion, your life, and your love, as it has become mine.

SUGGESTED READING

Rather than a detailed bibliography, which can get laboriously boring, I've included in this section a sampling of books and tapes which have been the most meaningful to me since beginning this journey. As I look over the list, there seems to be something for everyone, a little physics, a little philosophy, a little psychology, a little science, a little metaphysics, a little religion, and so on. If you want to dig deeper into this way of life, or if you just want to expand your knowledge in certain areas, follow your inner guidance, and you'll find what's right for you.

Alcoholics Anonymous, 1975. New York: Alcoholics Anonymous World Services, Inc.

Bailes, Frederick. 1971. *Your Mind Can Heal You.* rev. ed. New York: Dodd, Mead.

Bailey, Alice A. 1930. *The Soul and Its Mechanism (The Problem of Psychology).* New York: Lucis Publishing Co.

Bartholomew (Spirit). 1998. *From the Heart of a Gentle Brother.* Carlsbad, Calif.: Hay House.

Bartholomew (Spirit). 1997. *I Come as a Brother: A Remembrance of Illusions.* rev. ed. Edited by Joy Franklin, Mary-Margaret Moore, and Jill Kramer. Carlsbad, Calif.: Hay House.

Becker, Robert O., and Gary Selden. 1985. *The Body Electric: Electromagnetism and the Foundation of Life.* New York: Morrow.

Bentov, Itzhak. 1977. *Stalking the Wild Pendulum: On the Mechanics of Consciousness.* New York: E. P. Dutton.

Besant, Annie, and C. W. Leadbetter. 1999. *Thought-Forms.* 2d ed. Wheaton, Ill.: Quest Books.

Blavatsky, H. P. 1977. *The Secret Doctrine: The Synthesis of Science, Religion, and Philosophy.* 2 vols. Pasadena, Calif.: Theosophical University Press.

Bohr, Niehls. 1934. *Atomic Theory and the Description of Nature.* Cambridge, England: Cambridge University Press.

Brazier, Mary Agnes Burniston. 1968. *The Electrical Activity of the Nervous System. A Textbook for Students.* 3d ed. Baltimore, Md.: Williams and Wilkins.

Bucke, Richard Maurice. 1969. *Cosmic Consciousness: A Study in the Evolution of the Human Mind.* New York: Causeway Books.

Capra, Fritjof. 1976. *The Tao of Physics: An Exploration of the Parallels Between Modern Physics and Eastern Mysticism.* 3d ed. Boston, Mass.: Shambhala Publications.

Carey, Ken. 1991. *Starseed, the Third Millennium: Living in the Posthistoric World.* San Francisco, Calif.: HarperSanFrancisco.

Carey, Ken. 1991. *The Starseed Transmissions.* San Francisco, Calif.: HarperSanFrancisco.

Carey, Ken. 1985. *Vision.* Kansas City, Mo.: Uni-Sun.

Cooke, Maurice B. 1983. *Einstein Doesn't Work Here Anymore.* Toronto, Canada: Marcus Books.

Course in Miracles, A. 1999. Mill Valley, Calif.: Foundation for Inner Peace.

Diagram Group. 1982. *The Brain: A User's Manual.* New York: Putnam.

Emmanuel (Spirit). 1989. *Emmanuel's Book: A Manual for Living Comfortably in the Cosmos.* Compiled by Pat Rodegast and Judith Stanton. New York: Bantam Books.

Emmanuel (Spirit). 1989. *Emmanuel's Book II: The Choice for Love.* Compiled by Pat Rodegast and Judith Stanton. New York: Bantam Books.

Gawain, Shakti. 1978. *Creative Visualization*. Berkeley, Calif.: Whatever Pub.

Hay, Louise L. 1987. *You Can Heal Your Life*. Santa Monica, Calif.: Hay House.

Hilarion: by Cooke, Maurice. *Seasons of the Spirit*. 1979. Ontario, Canada: Marcus Books.

Hilarion: by Cooke, Maurice. *Symbols*. 1979. Ontario, Canada: Marcus Books.

Hill, Napoleon. 1966. *Think and Grow Rich*. New York: Hawthorn Books.

Hills, Christopher B. 1975. *Supersensonics: The Spiritual Physics of All Vibrations from Zero to Infinity*. Boulder Creek, Calif.: University of the Trees Press.

Holmes, Ernest. 1938. *The Science of Mind*. New York: R. M. McBride and Co.

Jung, C. G. 1966. *Collected Works*. Edited by Sir Herbert Read, Michael Fordham, and Gerhard Adler. London: Routledge and K. Paul.

King, Godfré Ray. 1982. *Unveiled Mysteries*. 4th ed. Schaumburg, Ill.: Saint Germain Press.

Lazaris. 1987. *The Sacred Journey, You and Your Higher Self*. Edited by Jach Pursel. Beverly Hills, Calif.: Concept: Synergy Publishing.

Lazaris: Awakening the Love. 1986. Edited by Jach Pursel. Beverly Hills, Calif.: Concept: Synergy Publishing. Videocassette.

Leadbetter, C. W. 1925. *Man Visible and Invisible.* Wheaton, Ill.: Theosophical Publishing House.

Leadbetter, C. W. 1927. *The Chakras.* Wheaton, Ill.: Theosophical Publishing House.

Maltz, Maxwell. 1960. *Psycho-Cybernetics: A New Way to Get More Living Out of Life.* Englewood Cliffs, N.J.: Prentice-Hall.

Murphy, Joseph. 1980. *How to Use the Laws of Mind.* Marina del Rey, Calif.: DeVorss and Co.

Ostrander, Sheila, and Lynn Schroeder. 1970. *Psychic Discoveries Behind the Iron Curtain.* Englewood Cliffs, N.J.: Prentice-Hall.

Peck, M. Scott, M.D. 1977. *The Road Less Traveled: A New Psychology of Love, Traditional Values, and Spiritual Growth.* New York: Simon and Schuster.

Powell, Arthur Edward. 1996. *The Etheric Double: The Health Aura.* Wheaton, Ill.: Quest Books.

Prophet, Mark, and Elizabeth Prophet. 1972. *Climb the Highest Mountain: The Everlasting Gospel.* Colorado Springs: Summit Lighthouse.

Ramtha: by Knight, J. Z. *Brain*, speciality audio tape A-23. 1982. Yelm, Wash.: Ramtha Dialogues.

Ramtha: by Knight, J. Z. *Superconsciousness*, video tape series. 1985. Yelm, Wash.: Ramtha Dialogues.

Ramtha. 1986. *Ramtha*. Edited by Steven Lee Weinberg with Randall Weischedel, Sue Ann Fazio, and Carol Wright. Eastsound, Wash.: Sovereignty, Inc.

Roberts, Jane. 1970. *The Seth Material*. Englewood Cliffs, N.J.: Prentice-Hall.

Seth (Spirit). 1972. *Seth Speaks: The Eternal Validity of the Soul*. Channeled by Jane Roberts. Englewood Cliffs, N.J.: Prentice-Hall.

Seth (Spirit). 1974. *The Nature of Personal Reality*. Notes by Robert F. Butts. Englewood Cliffs, N.J.: Prentice-Hall.

Troward, Thomas. 1909. *The Edinburgh Lectures on Mental Science*. New York: Roger Brothers.

Valentin, Ann. 1987. *Cosmic Revelation*. Channeled by Ann Valentin and Virginia Essene. Santa Clara, Calif.: S.E.E. Publishing Co.

Valentin, Ann. 1988. *Descent of the Dove*. Santa Clara, Calif.: S.E.E. Publishing Co.

Yogananda, Paramahansa. 1986. *The Divine Romance*. Los Angeles, Calif.: Self-Realization Fellowship.

INDEX

V
vacationing, 69
victim mentality, 20, 26-28

W
will, 49, 95-98
woodcutter story, 11

About the Author

Lynn Grabhorn is a long-time student of the way in which thought and feelings format our lives. Raised in Short Hills, New Jersey, she began her working life in the advertising field in New York City, founded and ran an audio-visual educational publishing company in Los Angeles, and owned and ran a mortgage brokerage firm in Washington State.

Lynn's books, including *Excuse Me, Your Life Is Waiting* and *The Excuse Me, Your Life Is Waiting Playbook* have received high acclaim from all corners of the world.

For more information, see Lynn's web page at www.lynn grabhorn.com

HAMPTON ROADS
PUBLISHING COMPANY, INC.

Thank you for reading *Beyond the Twelve Steps*. Hampton Roads is proud to publish the incomparable work of Lynn Grabhorn. Please take a look at the following selection or visit us anytime on the web: www.hrpub.com.

Excuse Me, Your Life Is Waiting
The Astonishing Power of Feelings
Lynn Grabhorn

Ready to get what you want? Get this: hard work and positive thinking can't do it alone. Lynn Grabhorn introduces you to "The Law of Attraction" and uncovers the hidden power of positive feeling. Now in paperback, this upbeat yet down-to-earth book reveals how our true feelings work to "magnetize" and create the reality we experience.

Discover the secrets that have made *Excuse Me* a *New York Times* **bestseller!**

Paperback • 320 pages • ISBN 1-57174-381-2 • $16.95

The Excuse Me, Your Life Is Waiting *Playbook*
With the 12 Tenets of Awakening

Lynn Grabhorn

This companion to *Excuse Me, Your Life Is Waiting* is a humorous and uplifting guide to awakening that offers witty stories, insightful graphics, and practical exercises that are actually FUN to do. However, don't be fooled, whether the Playbook is used by groups or individuals, its content and design will gently awaken and enhance the great Master in us all.

Paperback • 288 pages • ISBN 1-57174-270-0 • $22.95

Hampton Roads Publishing Company

. . . for the evolving human spirit

HAMPTON ROADS PUBLISHING COMPANY publishes books on a variety of subjects, including metaphysics, spirituality, health, visionary fiction, and other related topics.

For a copy of our latest trade catalog, call toll-free, 800-766-8009, or send your name and address to:

HAMPTON ROADS PUBLISHING COMPANY, INC.
1125 STONEY RIDGE ROAD • CHARLOTTESVILLE, VA 22902
e-mail: hrpc@hrpub.com • www.hrpub.com